S. Neil MacFarlane

Intervention in Contemporary World Politics

Adelphi Paper 350

Oxford University Press, Great Clarendon Street, Oxford OX2 6DP
Oxford   New York
Athens   Auckland   Bangkok   Bombay   Calcutta   Cape Town
Dar es Salaam   Delhi   Florence   Hong Kong   Istanbul   Karachi
Kuala Lumpur   Madras   Madrid   Melbourne   Mexico City
Nairobi   Paris   Singapore   Taipei   Tokyo   Toronto
and associated companies in
Berlin   Ibadan

Oxford is a trade mark of Oxford University Press

Published in the United States
by Oxford University Press Inc., New York

© The International Institute for Strategic Studies 2002

First published August 2002 by **Oxford University Press for
The International Institute for Strategic Studies**
Arundel House, 13–15 Arundel Street, Temple Place, London WC2R 3DX
www.iiss.org

Director John Chipman
Editor Mats R. Berdal
Assistant Editor Charles Hebbert

British Library Cataloguing in Publication Data
Data available

Library of Congress Cataloguing in Publication Data

ISBN 0-19-851678-9
ISSN 0567-932x

Contents

5   **Glossary**

7   **Introduction**

13   Chapter 1   **The Terms of the Debate**

19   Chapter 2   **Intervention in Pre-Cold War International History**
   - *Intervention in the Peloponnesian War 20*
   - *Intervention in pre-Westphalian Europe 21*
   - *The French Revolution and the Concert of Europe 23*
   - *Intervention in the interwar period 29*

33   Chapter 3   **Intervention during the Cold War**
   - *The normative dimension 33*
   - *The Cold War practice of intervention 38*

47   Chapter 4   **The Interlude of 'New Political Thinking'**

49   Chapter 5   **Post-Cold War Intervention**
   - *Post-Cold War normative developments 51*
   - *The post-Cold War practice of intervention 61*

77   **Conclusion**
   - *Afterword 81*

85   **Notes**

Glossary

ASEAN	Association of South-east Asian Nations
CIS	Commonwealth of Independent States
ECOWAS	Economic Community of West African States
EO	Executive Outcomes
EU	European Union
IFOR	Implementation Force
INTERFET	International Force for East Timor
ISI	Inter-Services Intelligence (Pakistan)
MPRI	Military Professional Resources Incorporated
MVD	*Ministerstvo Vnutrennykh Del* (Russian Ministry of Internal Affairs)
NATO	North Atlantic Treaty Organisation
NGO	Non-Governmental Organisation
OAS	Organisation of American States
OAU	Organisation of African Unity
ONUMOZ	United Nations Operation in Mozambique
OSCE	Organisation for Security and Cooperation in Europe
RPF	Rwanda Popular Front
SG	Secretary-General (UN)
SOAO	South Osset Autonomous Oblast
SWAPO	South-west Africa People's Organisation

TDR	Transdnestr Republic
UNAMIR	UN Assistance Mission in Rwanda
UNAVEM	United Nations Angola Verification Mission
UNDPKO	UN Department of Peacekeeping Operations
UNGOMAP	United Nations Good Offices Mission in Afghanistan and Pakistan
UNITAF	UN Task Force (Somalia)
UNOMIG	UN Observer Mission in Georgia
UNPROFOR	UN Protection Force (Croatia and Bosnia)
UNSC	UN Security Council
UNSCOM	UN Special Commission
UNTAC	United Nations Transitional Authority in Cambodia
UNTAG	United Nations Transition Assistance Group
USSR	Union of Soviet Socialist Republics

Introduction

States have traditionally employed a range of means to pursue their objectives in international relations. The most extreme is war – organised force exercised from outside in order to change the policies of an adversary or to destroy it. Less extreme is intervention – the coercive attempt to change the internal political balance of another state. This may take different forms: in order to remove an uncooperative or hostile government, one might support its domestic adversaries. Alternatively, the desire to preserve an allied or friendly government threatened by internal dissent might evoke external assistance to that government in its internal struggle.

This paper examines the place of intervention in contemporary world politics. It asks whether the role and nature of intervention has changed in the post-Cold War era, and, if so, in what ways. One key issue here is the extent to which intervention has been transformed from its traditional role as a vehicle for the promotion of the political interests of states into a mechanism for the promotion of purportedly universal norms. There are two aspects to the post-Cold War normative dimension of intervention. The first is the defence of human rights; in particular, to what extent is there evidence of an emerging solidarist[1] norm concerning humanitarian intervention to protect civilian populations threatened by civil war, to protect relief supplies and the personnel delivering them, or, more strongly, to coerce states and other parties involved in civil conflict to cease their violations of the individual and group rights of those living under their authority?

Rosalyn Higgins noted in the mid-1980s that: 'Human rights have shifted from being a matter traditionally of solely domestic concern into a matter of legitimate international concern'.[2] Nicholas Wheeler went further in a work published in 2000: 'Humanitarian claims were not accepted as a legitimate basis for the use of force in the 1970s but ... a new norm of UN-authorised intervention developed in the 1990s'.[3] Kofi Annan concurred, identifying a 'developing international norm in favour of intervention to protect civilians'.[4] Secondly, in a number of cases in the 1990s (e.g., Haiti in 1994 and Sierra Leone in 1997), interventions were ostensibly undertaken to restore democratic regimes that had fallen victim to military coups. It may be becoming legitimate for international actors to use force to promote particular forms of internal state arrangements.

Hedley Bull once noted the general presumption in international relations that intervention was wrong, in that it violated the normal jurisdiction of states.[5] The moral basis of the principle of non-intervention was summarised by Adam Roberts:

> *It provides clear guidelines for limiting the uses of armed force and reducing the risk of war between armies of different states. It involves respect for different societies with varying religions, cultures, economic systems and political arrangements. It acts as a brake on the crusading, territorial and imperial ambitions of states.*[6]

Bull and Roberts also recognised that most reasonable people would accept that in particular instances there might be compelling reasons to override this general presumption on normative or other grounds. The emergence of solidarist norms legitimating intervention would considerably broaden the category of exceptions and would correspondingly weaken the principle of non-intervention. In the extreme, it might be suggested that these solidarist concerns are displacing more political and self-interested considerations as motivations for interference in the domestic affairs of other states. The latter remain largely proscribed by the principle of non-intervention; the former may be gaining legal status and general acceptance in international society.

That this enhancement of the normative nature of intervention is considered a very important aspect of its evolution in the international system is evident in the burgeoning literature on the ethics and law of intervention. However, the normative dimension is only part of the broader question of the role of intervention as a political/military instrument that states use to pursue their perceived interests. Here one might ask whether the changing structural (and normative) conditions of the post-Cold War era altered states' predisposition to engage in intervention and the ways in which they did so. Finally, the discussion of intervention has been overwhelmingly focused on state practice and on the norms pertaining to states. Yet a number of other groups have emerged that engage in interventionist behaviour. Moreover, the activities of transnational groups, interventionist or not, may create new incentives for intervention. How has the emergence or growing significance of non-state (transnational or multilateral) actors in the post-Cold War era affected the practice of intervention and its significance in international politics? To put the matter more simply, has the development of the international system brought new or different answers to these questions:

1. who intervenes?
2. where do they intervene?
3. how do they intervene?
4. why do they intervene?

There are several possible approaches to a general discussion of intervention, including the legal, ethical, and political. As was noted above, the post-Cold War discussion of intervention has been dominated by the first two of these perspectives,[7] with particular reference to the concepts of sovereignty and humanitarian intervention. In legal analysis, what matters is the definition and elaboration of norms that are deemed to have the status of law and compliance with or in violation of these norms. As regards intervention, the key issue is whether and to what extent elements of international law might permit violation of the codified and customary rights of sovereign states. Discussion of the ethics of intervention focuses on the extent to which moral principles (e.g., the protection of human dignity) may serve as a legitimate basis for interference in the domestic affairs of states. In political analysis, what matters is the self-interested effort to influence the internal affairs of a state, either on behalf of a government and with the consent of recognised authorities or in opposition to a government and without consent; and the extent to which and ways in which states are motivated or constrained by normative frameworks in their definition of interest and policy choices regarding such intrusions.

One fundamental problem with the literature on intervention is that there are few efforts to merge legal and ethical with political perspectives. The different approaches proceed along parallel tracks with little cross-fertilisation. This paper recognises the importance of legal and ethical approaches to intervention. However, it seeks to situate these perspectives within a political logic, viewing intervention as a coercive application of power directed at modification of political processes or authority structures within other states. The motivations underlying intervention may be self-interested or they may reflect the pursuit of particular or general normative principles. Intervention proceeds in a legal and normative context that may (or may not) influence the conduct and frequency of intervention. But at its root, intervention is a political act and is considered as such here.

In pursuing these questions, the starting point is the definition of the principal terms of analysis. This is followed by a summary of the place of intervention in international history. The paper then turns to an examination of the normative context and the practical role of intervention in the international relations of the Cold War era. The third section analyses the evolution of the theory and practice of intervention after the Cold War. The paper concludes with a discussion of the implications of the analysis for assessing of the place of intervention in world politics.

The paper argues that the displacement of *raison d'état* by international norms is more apparent than real. Intervention in the 1990s and at the beginning of the new century continues to be motivated substantially by considerations of state and alliance interest. Where such interest is not perceived to be present, intervention tends not to occur, whatever the prevailing humanitarian situation. In this sense, intervention remains a fundamentally political form of behaviour.

Nonetheless, the political use of intervention appears to be constrained by two important factors that have emerged in the post-Cold War period. In the first place, although unilateral intervention against an established sovereign government was normatively (and legally) proscribed under the principle of non-intervention for much of the twentieth century, this had little effect on the practice of states during the Cold War. Competitive, unilateral, self-interested intervention was common practice for the two superpowers and for many other actors in world politics.

In contrast, in the post-Cold War period, such intervention is more rare (though hardly absent). Intervention increasingly occurs in a multilateral context, on the basis of authorisation by international organisations, above all the United Nations. The need to build support within such organisations in turn requires a greater degree of sensitivity to, and accommodation of, the perspectives of other states. This limits state flexibility to a degree. Of course, the Kosovo case suggests that the necessity of a mandate from the United Nations is not absolute. However, in this instance too, the United States situated its project within a multilateral context (NATO) and accepted a degree of consequent constraint on its behaviour in order to create and sustain consensus on its preferred course of action.

This leads to the second point. For intervention to be legitimately mandated, it must be justified in terms of normative principles that are generally accepted in international society. Although such justification may to some extent be spurious and mask power-political or other self-centred motivations, the need to justify again narrows the behavioural parameters of states.[8] To be seen to be acting in a manner inconsistent with the stated justification carries potential political costs. Hence, the principal motivation of French intervention in Rwanda in mid-1994 may have been political. At the international level, this amounted to the salvaging of a longstanding ally in the hope that France would continue to play a role in the politics of Central Africa. Domestically, the intervention was an attractive means for the Socialists to take the moral high ground in their impending electoral contest with the right. Nonetheless, the action took on a limited but effective humanitarian role and saved many people who otherwise might have perished. Elsewhere, had the United States sought to capitalise on the successful military campaign against the Federal Republic of Yugoslavia by pushing for Kosovar independence, it would have fractured its alliance while causing still greater difficulties in its relationship with Russia, China and the countries of the non-aligned movement. In this respect, perhaps the most significant aspect of the evolution of intervention in the 1990s has been not the emergence of new rationales for action, but the deepening of societal constraints on the practice of intervention.

However, as is discussed in an afterword to this paper, the American-led intervention in Afghanistan raises questions about this conclusion. Although the United States secured a multilateral mandate for its intervention in Afghanistan, its conduct of the campaign was largely unilateral. Its contemplation of follow-on action against Iraq betrayed little concern over multilateral frameworks for action. Its questioning of the applicability of the Geneva Convention to Taliban and al-Qaeda detainees raised doubts about the strength of normative constraints on the one remaining superpower when it perceives vital interests to be at stake.

Chapter 1

The Terms of the Debate

Discussion of the place of intervention in international politics presumes an understanding of what intervention is.[1] Different disciplines have differing views on this point. From a political perspective, intervention is an engagement in the domestic affairs of a state intended to change (or to preserve) the structure of power and authority within it. In attempting to influence the internal politics of another state, intervenors may use political, economic or military instruments. In general, however, discussion of intervention focuses on military action. In legal discourse on intervention, the focus is on military action that is not requested and is not approved by the authorities of a state.[2] Hence, for example, the 1964 French deployment to Gabon 'to put down an uprising led by the leader of the opposition party'[3] would not, in a legal sense, be an intervention.

This may be appropriate in the consideration of the permissibility or non-permissibility in law of a particular intrusion. From a political perspective, however, the focus is the influence on domestic political balances and outcomes. Military engagement may or may not be consensual, but the concept of intervention generally implies a coercive act. When a government invites or consents to intervention, it is with the intention that military means from outside be used to coerce their domestic adversaries. When an opposition movement acts likewise, it is with similar intent and, generally, consequences. This understanding of the term reflects common usage outside legal circles. In the paper cited earlier, for example, although France acted at the request of the recognised government of Gabon, Chipman refers to the French action as an intervention. The French called the unit they developed for such support of incumbent governments the *Force d'intervention armée.*[4]

The problems with such a definition are obvious. At what moment does military assistance to a government become intervention? The provision of arms and training in how to use them may be as, or more effective than, the dispatch of combat units. Economic and financial pressure can be as effective in modifying the domestic policies of a government, or in causing that government to fall, as military action. Propaganda can also have an important effect on the internal political process of a target country. The failure to act can have consequences for the domestic political balance of a target country that are as significant as those of an act of intervention. It is for reasons such as these that Stanley Hoffmann once observed that:

> The subject [intervention] is practically the same as that of international politics in general from the beginning of time to the present ... Anything can constitute an intervention, indeed even non-acts can constitute intervention.[5]

Recognising these problems, this analysis focuses on the direct and coercive application of military force in internal conflicts to affect their course and outcome, since this appears to be the undisputed core of the issue of intervention. The element of coercion in the definition is necessary to differentiate intervention from the plethora of other actions taken by states or multilateral organisations to influence the internal affairs of other states.[6] The stress on military interference distinguishes intervention from other forms of coercive pressure on states (e.g., sanctions and conditionality).

If one sees intervention to be a coercive application of force intended to affect domestic political processes and outcomes, then it is not immediately clear whether intervention for explicitly normative purposes falls within the category. On the face of it, humanitarian intervention is intended to protect civilians rather than to affect domestic political balances. However, the application of coercion is frequently designed to alter the behaviour of politico-military actors through compulsion or deterrence; it can have the effect of constraining or enabling particular parties to civil conflicts; and, in extreme circumstances, it may reflect the judgement that political change is necessary to achieve humanitarian ends. More-over, as we shall see below, 'governmental involvement in humanitarian action owed much to political considerations that were often tinged with an element of *realpolitik*'.[7] For all of these reasons, humanitarian intervention is considered to be consistent with the definitional focus of this paper.

There are also clear difficulties in defining the boundary between intervention (coercive military interference in the internal affairs of another state) and war (military conflict between states). Classification of an action as intervention or war depends in considerable measure on the perspective from which it is being viewed. As one analyst put it: 'Regarded from the point of view of the state intruded upon, it [intervention] must always remain an act which, if not consented to, is an act of war.'[8] An act's status as intervention may also depend on how one perceives the threat to which it is a response. In the case of South Vietnam, for example, to the extent that the challenge to the political status quo in Vietnam was an insurrection on the part of the Vietcong, US action qualifies as intervention; if one views it to have been North Vietnamese aggression, then it was war. And action in South Vietnam spilled over in 1964–65 into air war against the North Vietnamese states.

NATO action in Kosovo is frequently considered to be intervention, and, in the sense that it was a response to Serb treatment of the Albanian minority in that region of the Federal Republic of Yugoslavia through assistance to that minority, it was. None the less, it involved a direct attack on another state from outside, which looks very much like war. This would suggest that, in practice, there is no clear line between the two.

Discussion of the concept of intervention is tightly linked to the question of sovereignty. The traditional understanding of sovereignty is that states have jurisdiction (some would say absolute jurisdiction) over their territory and that, because states are legally equal members of an international society that lacks a supreme authority, this jurisdiction is recognised by other states. This understanding is the basis for the principle of non-intervention.

However, one should recognise that this principle is diluted in some aspects of the legal and ethical discussion of intervention. Consideration of the issue dates back at least to the work of Grotius in the seventeenth century. In the nineteenth century, as will be seen below, there was much discussion amongst statesmen of the desirability of intervention for humanitarian purposes. The question arose in the context of the Greek war of independence (1821–1830), where decisive Anglo-French and Russian intervention was justified in part by the cruelty of the Ottomans towards their Greek subjects. It appeared again in the 1870s with reference to Ottoman treatment of subject populations in the Balkans.[9] These cases are arguably early manifestations of a solidarist critique of international pluralism in which it is asserted that there are certain universal values, the defence and promotion of which is more important than the defence of sovereignty as a constitutive principle of international society.[10] For those holding this view, it follows that in cases where these values are violated in a systematic fashion, other states have a right to intervene to stop the actions in question. This would imply that sovereignty is limited and conditional, rather than absolute. Consideration of conditions placed upon sovereignty in the 1990s produced the notion of 'sovereignty as responsibility'.[11] From this perspective, the extent of a state's sovereignty depends on the manner in which that state conducts its relations with its citizens.

The final point to mention concerns the actors (who intervenes?). The initiator of an act of intervention has traditionally been the state,[12] although the recipient of assistance may be either an incumbent government or its non-state adversaries. In the twentieth century, however, the cast has broadened. The activities of Comintern in Germany and China in the 1920s and Spain in the 1930s raised the possibility that transnational political movements might also engage in intervention, although the close ties between Comintern and the Soviet communist party and state raised legitimate doubts about the degree to which the organisation was anything more than a non-traditional extension of state policy.

The post-Cold War era has provided possibly clearer examples of the interventionist role of non-state and transnational actors in world politics. One variant is private military companies, which have intervened in a number of civil conflicts, supporting governments in return for profit.[13] Another is al-Qaeda, which, during the 1990s, played a significant financial and military role in supporting the Taliban effort to consolidate control over Afghanistan. In return, al-Qaeda received sanctuary in a sympathetic environment.

In turn, the activities of these transnational movements have at times provoked varying degrees of intervention on the part of states threatened by their activities. In the last stages of the Cold War, Manuel Noriega's connections to international drug cartels provided one reason for American intervention in Panama to overthrow him. Colombia's role as a venue for narcotics trafficking, and the links between traffickers and opposition guerrilla movements, provided the Clinton administration with a strong motivation to grant substantial military assistance to the Colombian government in its civil war. And the al-Qaeda attack on New York and Washington in September 2001 provoked American intervention in Afghanistan to overthrow the Taliban. The emergence of non-state actors as significant elements in the practice of intervention and of transnational groups and processes as factors motivating the interventionist behaviour of states raises questions about the utility of a purely state-centric focus in the study of intervention and about the adequacy of statist legal/normative frameworks related to intervention.[14]

The second category of non-state actor taking an increasingly significant role is that of international institutions. The role of such organisations was minimal prior to the twentieth century. Their capacity to exercise effective security roles during the Cold War was greatly constrained by the bipolar division in world politics and – more fundamentally – by the reluctance of states to cede responsibility and power to them. In the period prior to the end of the Cold War, there were very few instances of intervention by such organisations. Nor did these bodies have much practical significance in the provision of mandates. The post-Cold War era witnessed substantial change in both regards. The United Nations and multilateral regional organisations (e.g., the Commonwealth of

Independent States (CIS), the Economic Community of West African States (ECOWAS), and the North Atlantic Treaty Organisation (NATO)) became heavily involved both in mandating and in implementing interventions.

Chapter 2

Intervention in Pre-Cold War International History

In the chapters that follow, this paper examines the evolving normative framework of intervention and juxtaposes that framework with the politics and practice of intrusion into the internal affairs of other states. The current wisdom is that international society is moving from a reasonably unequivocal embrace of the principle of non-intervention to a situation where this principle (and the attendant understanding of sovereignty) can be attenuated in the face of violations of other norms (e.g., human rights) by states. From a historical perspective, the reality is much more complex. Periods of normative consensus regarding intervention have been interspersed with periods of intense disagreement. There has been considerable variation concerning the strength of the principle of non-intervention, ranging from its near absence in classical Greece and pre-Westphalian Europe through its emphatic embrace during much of the post-Second World War era of de-colonisation. In periods where the principle of non-intervention was contested, one sees a marked variety in normative justifications for overriding it. One recurring historical variant is the conservative argument that political change within a state might threaten legitimate political order in others (during the period of the Holy Alliance in the nineteenth century or during the Cold War). Another is the liberal argument that democracy within states is conducive to order among them (as was argued by Woodrow Wilson and later democratic peace theorists). A second liberal qualification of the principle of non-intervention is that intervention might be justified by the principle of national self-determination (the debate over apartheid). A third is that massive violation of the rights of citizens deprives the offending states of the protection of non-intervention norms (the current doctrine of humanitarian intervention).

There is also considerable variation over time in the frequency of intervention in practice. In some periods, intervention was rare (e.g., Europe in the first years after the Treaty of Westphalia); in others it was endemic (e.g., the early nineteenth century or the Cold War). Finally, there is great variation in the degree to which norms regarding intervention were reflected in practice. For much of the eighteenth century, for example, practice appeared to reflect normative principles rather closely. In the Cold War, by contrast, the strengthening normative constraint on intervention apparently existed in a world largely removed from the practical calculations and the behaviour of states.

There is little evidence of unilinearity or historical progression in this matter. What does seem clear is that the understanding and practice of intervention are strongly influenced by the changing political context of international relations.

Intervention in the Peloponnesian War

Taking Thucydides's account of the Peloponnesian War as a point of departure, the competitive intrusions into Epidamnus's domestic political struggle by Corcyra and Corinth provide an elegant early example of several distinctly modern dimensions of the politics of intervention.[1] In the first place, the system in which these interventions occurred was a pluralistic one linked together by certain societal bonds and characterised by a tendency towards bipolarity. In both respects, it resembled the mid-twentieth century international system.[2] Both poles in the system were deeply sensitive to slight changes in patterns of alliance. By extension, they were sensitive to internal changes in other states that might destabilise the pattern of alignment.

The democratic and aristocratic parties to the civil conflict in Epidamnus sought to manipulate the systemic rivalry in order to strengthen their position in the internal struggle for power. External powers were receptive to the appeals of local parties because of their perception that the outcome of the internal struggle was relevant to the broader international structure of power in which they operated. The potential escalatory dynamic of competitive intervention was manifest; what began as a struggle inside Epidamnus continued as a conflict between Corcyra and Corinth. This in turn drew in Athens, and the Corinthian defeat caused Corinth to turn to Sparta.

Thucydides's discussion of intervention had little normative content. There is in the relevant text some question as to whether Corinth had the right to interfere in the affairs of a city – Epidamnus – that had been colonised by Corcyra. But there is no questioning of the legitimacy of intervention in general. The image of international politics here focused on power and not principle. The central role of power, as opposed to justice and rights, is even more starkly posed in the Melian dialogue. Here, the Athenian representatives justified their demand for Melian accession to the Athenian Empire in the face of appeals for moderation and recognition of Melian neutrality as follows: 'You know as well as we do that, when these matters are discussed by practical people, the standard of justice depends on the equality of power to compel and that in fact the strong do what they have the power to do and the weak accept what they have to accept'.[3]

Intervention in pre-Westphalian Europe

Perhaps the most intense period of intervention in the history of the European states system was during the lead-up to the Peace of Westphalia in 1648, when a pluralistic system of sovereign states gradually began to re-emerge out of medieval Europe.[4] The growing competition between nascent sovereign powers was exacerbated by the Reformation. In the century-long process that culminated in the Thirty Years War (1618–1648), intervention was a major instrument in the hegemonic struggle between France and Germany, and the parallel struggle between Protestantism and Catholicism. France intervened to frustrate Charles V's effort to suppress Germany's Protestant princes in the mid-sixteenth century. Spain, England and the Dutch then intervened in France's religious wars. England subsequently intervened to support a revolt of the Dutch in the Spanish Netherlands.

Habsburg exhaustion brought a brief interlude at the beginning of the seventeenth century. However, the struggle soon resumed, focusing this time on Germany. The Thirty Years War
began with a Habsburg effort to suppress a revolt by Bohemia's
Protestant princes in 1618. This brought counter-intervention by
the Dutch, the Danes and then the Swedes, supported financially
by France. The widening challenge to Austria brought in Spain in
the 1630s. This in turn provoked direct intervention by France and
a widening of the war into France.

The combination of French, Swedish, and Dutch land action
against the Habsburgs in Central Europe, Dutch sea raids against
Spain's colonial possessions, revolts in Catalonia and Portugal (the
latter assisted by the English) and the gradual deterioration of
Spain's financial position once again drove the Habsburgs to peace.
They recognised the independence of the Dutch in 1648. Austria
settled with the German Protestants in the Peace of Westphalia,
signed in the same year. This left the conflict between France and
Spain, which was in turn settled in the Treaty of the Pyrenees in
1659.

This sequence of intervention and war reflected the fact that
the European system of the late sixteenth and early seventeenth
century was in transition from its late-feudal model of organisation, in which plurality was combined with hierarchy, to its
Westphalian variant, in which states were recognised as legally
equal and sovereign.[5] As in the Peloponnesian War, intervention
played a substantial part in the conduct of the larger hegemonic
struggle. What began as a quasi-domestic struggle (the Habsburg
effort to subdue the Bohemian Protestant Estates) drew in first one
circle of external powers (the Netherlands, Denmark, Sweden and
Spain). The arrival of the Spanish produced direct intervention by
the other principal pole of power – France.

Again, as in the Classical Greek case discussed above, prior to
and during the Thirty Years War there was little evidence of
normative resistance to intervention. In their intrusions into the
internal affairs of their neighbours, it was not obvious that the
great powers were contravening normative principles. The weakly
embedded quality of the principle of non-intervention reflected the
hierarchical notions characteristic of the late Middle Ages and the

interpenetrated conception of sovereignty characteristic of the period prior to the consolidation of absolutist monarchies and nation states. One might go further to suggest that intervention – far from being proscribed – was normatively justified on religious grounds. There appeared to be little questioning of the proposition that it was legitimate for states to interfere in the affairs of other states in order to promote their particular view of Christian universalism.

The outcome of the war was the termination of the Habsburg bid for hegemony in Europe and the crystallisation of a pluralist system in Europe. This formed the core of an international system that expanded eventually to a global level. The damage and the cost associated with the Thirty Years War were such that the major players in the international system concurred that issues and processes within countries were off limits. International relations became what went on between states rather than within them.[6] This was expressed normatively in the principle of *cuius rex, eius religio*, to the effect that each ruler could decide his state's own religion. Importantly, in terms of the discussion of the place of individual rights in the evolving politics of intervention, this right of choice was not extended to the subjects of particular rulers. Although the possibility that the principle of non-intervention could be relaxed on humanitarian grounds was discussed among international lawyers,[7] this view did not obviously affect state practice during the century that followed the Thirty Years War.

The French Revolution and the Concert of Europe

It took the French Revolution and its Napoleonic aftermath to bring into question once again the normative dimension of intervention. These events highlighted how change within a major state could be destabilising to the system as a whole. The French revolutionaries, at least initially, saw their security to be tied to the internal transformation of their neighbours. In 1792, the Convention declared its commitment to providing 'fraternity and assistance to all peoples who shall wish to recover their independence'. It then asked the Executive to give orders to its generals 'to furnish assistance to these peoples'. France's adversaries naturally saw their security to be tightly tied to the internal transformation (restoration) of France. In this respect, the period of the French Revolution and the Napoleonic Wars is symptomatic of Vincent's observation that 'a revolutionary international system, in which revisionist movements challenge the status quo might likewise be a greater encouragement to intervention than a system composed of satisfied conservative powers'.[8]

One sees the effects of the French Revolution on thinking about intervention clearly in the works of Lord Brougham, who initially defended a norm of 'inviolable independence'. In the face of the French Revolution, he came to accept that intervention might be necessary in the face of 'a great and manifest, and also an immediate danger':

> *Whenever a sudden and great danger takes place in the internal structure of a State, dangerous in a high degree to all neighbours, they have a right to attempt, by hostile interference, the restoration of an order of things safe unto themselves ... The right can only be deemed competent in cases of sudden and great aggrandisement, such as that of France in 1790, endangering the safety of the neighbouring powers.*[9]

Not surprisingly, after the ending of Napoleon's challenge to the pluralism of the European system in 1815 there was considerable tension between the effort to re-establish the pluralist principle with its associated understanding of sovereignty and the desire on the part of conservative great powers to sustain order through forceful intervention in the internal affairs of states. Two major Concert powers (Austria and Russia) argued strongly that intervention to protect conservative monarchies against republicanism and liberal revolution was a necessary and legitimate element of the management of international order. In this view, the purpose of the Concert of Europe was not only the regulation of the international behaviour of states, but the preservation of internal structures that were perceived to be conducive to stability in the system as a whole. Together the two states produced a proposal for a Holy Alliance, dedicated to the reversal of the achievements of revol-

ution in Europe, and the prevention of further revolutionary up-
heavals.[10]

In short, for some of the great powers at least, there was a
normative basis for intervention in the domestic affairs of other
states, although it was evident that the norm in question served the
purpose of protecting the positions of conservative monarchs. In
this respect, the Holy Alliance's justification of intervention was
the negation of the solidarist principles that have come to play
such a significant role in the discussion of intervention in the late
twentieth century. Intervention was justified in terms of the need
to preserve order through the suppression of popular challenges to
the status quo, and the denial of what have come to be seen as
universal human rights.

In contrast, the British government (and Parliament) was
distinctly unenthusiastic about the idea of a generalised norm of
intervention against revolution. Castlereagh argued forcefully
against a norm of general interference, not only because this was in
his view contrary to English law, but also because it might become
a recipe for 'universal tyranny' in the hands of 'less beneficent
monarchs'. However, this was not so much a defence of the
principle of non-intervention as it was a questioning of the Holy
Alliance rationale for intervention. Castlereagh noted Britain did
not oppose intervention *per se*, and, following Brougham, had
occasionally found it useful in self-defence.[11]

Such acts, however, were not based on a 'generalised right'.
Instead, they were exceptional and could not be considered to
reflect a rule of international conduct.[12] Disagreement over the
place of intervention in international relations was one element
of a broader tension between liberalism and conservatism in
European politics.[13] However, both sides in this debate accepted
the status of intervention as a useful and legitimate instrument in
the pursuit of political objectives (self-defence on the one hand and
containing revolutionary contagion on the other).

Two other elements of the normative discussion of intervention in this period should be stressed. The first concerns the
legitimacy of intervention outside the European society of states.
Non-European states for the most part were not considered equal
members of international society. They were consequently not

protected by Westphalian norms of non-intervention. As Gerrit Gong put it:

> In the minds of international lawyers, 'civilisation' became a scale by which the countries of the world were categorized into 'civilised', barbarous, and savage spheres. The legal rights and duties of states in each sphere were based on the legal capacity their degree of 'civilisation' supposedly entitled them to possess ... Civilised states alone were qualified to be recognized with full international legal status and personality, full membership in the Family of Nations, and full protection in international law.[14]

In general, the European powers took the view that intervention outside Europe to protect their citizens or property was their right. Intervention and, for that matter, the broader project of European colonialism were justified in a more profound sense by ideas of European superiority and of Europe's *mission civilisatrice*.[15]

The second concerns humanitarian intervention, an issue that arose first and foremost in the Concert's consideration of the growing instability in the European possessions of the Ottoman Empire. The case displays eloquently the tension between pluralist and solidarist norms, between conservative (order-based) and liberal (justice-based) principles of intervention, and the interweaving of politics with principle that is so characteristic of the modern practice of humanitarian intervention. The core issue was the gradual Ottoman loss of control over their possessions in the Balkans, starting in a revolt in the Danubian Principalities in 1821, extending to Greece in the same year, and then on to Bosnia and Bulgaria later in the century. The region was an area in which Austrian and Russian interests intersected, giving both powers strong (and potentially conflicting) concerns over the outcome of the process. Matters were further complicated by Ottoman violence against the Christian population of the region, many of whom shared Russia's Orthodox confession.

Those rebelling against the Ottomans appealed to the tsar on religious grounds to rescue them from the Turks. Alexander I was strongly tempted to intervene in 1821. Austria, in contrast, strongly opposed intervention, having declared the preservation of the Ottoman Empire in the Balkans to be a matter of strategic interest. Prince Metternich ultimately dissuaded Alexander from intervention, arguing that the Balkan events were a distraction from the major threat in Europe – ascendant liberalism.[16] Metternich was joined in the effort to restrain Russia by Castlereagh. For Britain, Russian territorial expansion towards the Mediterranean and the Levant was anathema. Castlereagh's admonition to the tsar concerning non-intervention is symptomatic of the nineteenth-century statesman's view of order versus justice in international relations:

> *Castlereagh did not deny that the atrocities committed by the Turks 'made humanity shudder'. But, like Metternich, he insisted that humanitarian considerations were subordinate to maintaining the 'consecrated structure' of Europe, which would be jarred to the core by any radical innovation.*[17]

The Greek War dragged on, however, and in 1827 Britain, France, and Russia coerced the Ottoman Empire into accepting Greek independence. As Wheeler points out, the humanitarian logic was central to the justification of this line of policy.[18] What is important here, however, is that the political constraints on what was ostensibly a humanitarian intervention had shifted dramatically in a permissive direction.[19] The ensuing years had seen an increase in the links between British and French liberals and the Greek rebels and the growth of a considerable sympathy in Europe for the plight of the Greeks, as typified by Lord Byron's fatal journey to Greece. The emergence of a substantial domestic political constituency supporting Greek independence in both France and Britain altered the calculations of leaders in both countries. Links between British and French sympathisers and the Greek independence movement also reduced the likelihood that an independent Greece would be dependent on Russia, hence reducing the British strategic interest in sustaining Ottoman power there. To put it another way, this had become a liberal project of self-determination, rather than an Orthodox project of defending the faithful.

There were also clear power-political calculations behind this shift in policy. Britain's foreign policy establishment, now under Canning, had concluded that Russian aspirations in Greece could be more effectively controlled through cooperation than through confrontation. In addition, British opposition to the Holy Alliance had stiffened under Canning. Given continuing Austrian opposition to intervention in the Ottoman Empire, cooperation with the Russians was seen as a means of weakening the Alliance by driving a wedge between its two principal adherents. Finally, commercial considerations also intruded; the failure of the Turks to protect British commerce was another factor motivating the British shift of position. Though one would not wish to deny the significance of the humanitarian dimension of intervention,[20] the actions of outside powers in the Greek War of Independence illustrate the strong element of politico–strategic interest in decisions by states to defend the rights of other oppressed populations, a theme that recurs in the late twentieth century in the consideration of humanitarian intervention. The Greeks deployed humanitarian arguments (and confessional ones) to secure external support in their bid for independence. The Russians were tempted to respond for reasons of prestige and longstanding strategic interest in the Balkans. The attitude of the other major players was driven to a considerable degree by their concern over the balance of power in Europe.

More generally, the practice of the Concert period within Europe reflected the weakness of the principle of non-intervention and the influence of the conservative norms mentioned above. Intervention played a key role in the strategies of the European great powers in the first half of the nineteenth century in areas where their interests were perceived to be at stake, and where others were either unwilling or unable to oppose them. Austria intervened forcibly to suppress revolutions in Naples and the Piedmont in 1821, and in Modena and Parma in 1831, thereby consolidating Vienna's pre-eminence in Italy.[21] Spain and Portugal were the scene of repeated competing interventions in the 1820s, as liberals and conservatives battled for power in both countries. Twenty years later – in an instance where British and French interests were not in play – Nicholas I dispatched an army of 120,000 men to crush the Hungarian revolution of 1848.

Outside Europe, intervention by the European great powers was also frequent and even less constrained by the principle of non-intervention or, to judge from the various atrocities of the period, by broader concerns about human rights. The same was true of the deepening engagement of the United States in the Caribbean Basin after the American Civil War that culminated in Theodore Roosevelt's corollary to the Monroe Doctrine.[22] The Americans intervened to secure the removal of Spain from its remaining possessions in the region, to create the state of Panama, to ensure repayment of debt by Santo Domingo and to defend and promote American economic interests in Mexico.[23] The American agenda in the region in the first two decades of the twentieth century focused on 'the virtue of order, the evil of revolution, and the benefits of North American – as opposed to foreign or European – enterprises'.[24] Where these were challenged, the United States frequently intervened to restore them. The Monroe Doctrine, the Roosevelt Corollary and Wilson's policy towards Mexico suggested that, from an American perspective, the sovereignty of other states in the region was limited and depended on the degree to which they abided by standards imposed by the United States. Like that of European states, America's doctrine of intervention focused again on matters of perceived interest (and notably the US desire to dominate the region, to prevent the engagement of extra-regional powers and to extract resources efficiently). Larger normative considerations played little role. The one exception was the intervention in Mexico, which had a democratising flavour. However, as Walter LaFeber noted, since the United States had no problem with other non-democratic governments in the region, there is reason to doubt the element of democratisation as a motivating factor in American action in Mexico.[25]

Intervention in the interwar period

The end of the First World War brought a number of significant normative changes of relevance to intervention in international politics. The embrace of the principle of self-determination in Woodrow Wilson's Fourteen Points and, subsequently, in attenuated form in the Treaty of Versailles introduced the possibility that the rights of non-sovereign peoples might be a legitimate object of international attention and – *in extremis* – intervention, prefiguring later debates regarding the legitimacy of intervention on behalf of national self-determination. The minority provisions of the post-First World War settlement were significant in qualifying sovereignty on the basis of universal rights to a limited degree. The League of Nations mandates system, in a rather diminutive way, recognised the rights both of colonial peoples and of international society with respect to German colonies that were transferred to the administration of one or other victorious power.

The outcome of the war also introduced a renewal of normative debate over the legitimacy of intervention. The Russian Revolution of October 1917 produced a revolutionary power in Europe that consciously rejected the norms of international society – including the inadmissibility of intervention, even in the limited form that it then took – and which was (rhetorically at least) committed to their overthrow. As Vincent put it:

> The principle of non-intervention might find a place in French revolutionary thought as the desirable norm in a world of national, popularly sovereign states; in Russian revolutionary doctrine, which had substituted class for nation, it appeared to find no place at all.[26]

Initially, the leaders of Soviet Russia perceived their very survival to hinge on the promotion of proletarian revolution in the major capitalist states, a perception heightened considerably by the Entente powers' intervention in Russia, first in the attempt to restore the eastern front and then, once the war ended, to reverse Russia's socialist revolution.[27] Ultimately, however, the experience of intervention in Russia's civil war encouraged the emergence of an intensely legalistic understanding of sovereignty and non-intervention on the part of Soviet scholars and decision-makers, and a corresponding weakening of their support for revolutionary movements abroad. Indeed, as early as 1919, in accepting the Entente powers' invitation to a meeting on Russia at Prinkipo, the new Soviet government agreed to include in any agreement with the allied powers 'an undertaking not to interfere in their internal affairs'.

The USSR quickly retreated from its global revolutionary pretensions into an essentially statist foreign policy. Where the Soviet Union did intervene in domestic disputes (as in Germany in 1923, China in 1923–27 and Spain in 1936–1939), these intrusions appeared to have far more to do with leadership interpretation of the Soviet state's (or their own personal) interest than with revolutionary normative commitments. In the first instance, Soviet and Comintern support of the German left's challenge to Gustav Stresemann followed closely on the latter's decision to remove the obstacles to a rapprochement with France and the UK, thereby threatening the incipient Soviet–German alliance of have-nots. The second involved an effort to create a Chinese nationalist counter to expanding Japanese and residual British influence along the USSR's Asian frontier. And in the third, support for the Spanish republicans was a means of diverting and tying down the growing threat from Germany, while providing Soviet agents with the opportunity to extinguish a communist faction loyal to Stalin's nemesis, Leon Trotsky.

Recalling the questions posed in the introduction, the pre-Cold War history of intervention was one in which political interest dominated as a cause of intervention. Intervention was seen as an instrument in the political struggle between states and groups of states. In this respect, as a method of seeking relative gains at the expense of adversaries, it was a replacement for, and often a supplement to, war.

At times, intervention had an important normative content. In the Thirty Years War, in the period of the Holy Alliance and in the inter-war period, intervention reflected normative or ideological preference (Protestantism versus Catholicism, liberalism versus conservatism, communism and socialism versus fascism). In these cases, however, the ideological dimension was closely tied to the power-political. The interweaving of motivations makes it difficult to assess the causal weight of normative propositions. With the exception of the intervention in the nineteenth century on behalf of the Christian subjects of the Ottoman Empire, there was little evidence of any serious consideration of the liberal solidarist norms that have been so prominent in discussion of intervention in the post-Cold War period. And a closer examination of that example reveals once again the close connection between normative arguments and political interests and the insufficiency of humanitarian motives alone to produce coercive action.

Finally, the variability in the influence of the principle of non-intervention is clear. With the possible exception of the late seventeenth and early and mid-eighteenth centuries, it was always contested to varying degrees by the practice, and sometimes by the normative arguments, of important players in the international system. In this respect, the normative challenge to the principle of non-intervention is nothing particularly new.

Chapter 3

Intervention during the Cold War

Even though the international system was divided into two profoundly hostile camps during the Cold War, the costs and risks of total war, and the dubious rationality of great power war as an option of policy, discouraged direct military confrontation between them. This effect was strengthened considerably by the presence of nuclear weapons and the emerging concept of mutual assured destruction. The limits on war as an instrument of policy enhanced the role of intervention as a means of altering or preserving the distribution of power in the system. Intervention was frequently used by both superpowers to sustain their spheres of influence (e.g., Hungary, the Dominican Republic, Czechoslovakia, and Grenada). Moreover, since the superpowers were in intense power-political competition but were reluctant to risk total war, intervention provided a potentially attractive means to pursue relative gains, principally in the 'grey zones' of the Third World.[1]

The normative dimension

Turning first to the normative dimension of Cold War intervention, it is curious that both solidarist conceptions of human rights and the responsibilities of states and the international community, on the one hand, and the pluralist conception of state sovereignty and the associated principle of non-intervention, on the other, grew in strength during the period. The Charter of the United Nations evinces a strong concern for individual and collective human rights, as well as some indication of UN and member-state obligations to promote these rights. Three years later, in 1948, the members of the General Assembly unanimously adopted the Universal Declaration of Human Rights.[2] The Declaration was followed in the 1960s by the Conventions on Civil and Political and on Economic and Social Rights. Ten years later, these conventions came into force after ratification by the requisite number of states. That is to say, there was a slow, but clear movement during the Cold War to recognise and elaborate the status of human rights as an international, rather than purely domestic, issue, and to give these rights force in international relations. This evolution implicitly challenged the absoluteness of the principle of non-intervention.[3]

International humanitarian law developed in the same direction. In 1977, the 'Protocol Additional to the Geneva Conventions of 12 August 1949, and Relating to the Protection of Victims on Non-International Armed Conflict (Protocol II)' extended the principles of protection of civilians in international war to civil wars, implying once again a diminution of state sovereignty in terms of the human rights of citizens.[4] In signing the protocol, states accepted internationally defined limitations on their internal behaviour. Many other international (e.g., the Convention on the Prevention and Punishment of Genocide[5]) and regional (e.g., the European Convention on Human Rights[6] and the American Convention on Human Rights[7]) treaty instruments of the Cold War era pushed international society in the same direction. The European Convention, although not of universal application, envisaged an important derogation of the sovereignty of signatories, particularly of those who accepted the obligatory jurisdiction of the European Court. In short, the evolution of legal instruments concerning human rights during the Cold War arguably established a substantial legal foundation for considering states' treatment of their citizens as a matter of international concern, arguably expanding the solidarist space in international relations and potentially providing some normative basis for rights-based intervention.[8]

Ironically, however, this expansion in the international dimension of human rights was accompanied by a contraction in the legal scope for intervention itself. Returning to the UN Charter, one finds Article 2 (1), which declares that the organisation is based on the principle of sovereign equality of states; Article 2 (4) which declares that all members of the UN are obliged to 'refrain from the threat or use of force against the territorial integrity or political independence of any State'; and Article 2 (7), which notes that 'nothing contained in the present Charter shall authorise the UN to intervene in matters which are essentially within the domestic jurisdiction of any state ...'.

The last article, however, contained an important reservation: that this principle did not prejudice the capacity of the Security Council to act under Chapter VII (Action with Respect to Threats to the Peace, Breaches of the Peace, and Acts of Aggression). The significance of this caveat was limited during the Cold War. Although threats to the peace were not defined in the Charter, it was none the less evident that the interpretation of the Charter during the Cold War focused on threats or acts of inter-state aggression, and not on threats emanating from domestic processes within states.[9] Moreover, given bipolarity and members' power of veto, the council had little capacity to act coercively against threats to international peace and security. Its capacity to extend the definition of threat in order to permit a response to crises within states or to the systematic violation of human rights by a recognised government was still more limited.[10]

Other acts of the United Nations General Assembly and of regional organisations such as the Organisation of African Unity (OAU) and the Organisation of American States (OAS) also contributed to the apparent legal absolutisation of sovereignty and the equally absolute proscription of intervention. The General Assembly's Declaration on Intervention (1965) began by asserting that no state had a right to intervene, directly or indirectly, in the internal or external affairs of another state. It continued by declaring that armed intervention was equivalent to aggression. Five years later, in the Declaration on Friendly Relations and Cooperation, the Assembly repeated this unequivocal position. The 8th preambulary paragraph insists that intervention, in whatever form, is a violation of the letter and the spirit of the Charter.[11] These acts of the General Assembly reflected the emergence of an ever-larger grouping of post-colonial states seeking to protect their independence. Since many were also weak, they sought normative protection in establishing and preserving their sovereignty. The emergence of this group of states continues to act as a significant brake on the capacity to widen the scope for legitimate intervention within the UN context.

Relevant judgements of the International Court of Justice during the Cold War also contributed to the strengthening of the principle of non-intervention.[12] For example, the Court's opinion in the Corfu Channel case (1949) amounts to a near-complete rejection of the legality of acts of intervention:

> *[The Court] can only regard the alleged right of intervention as the manifestation of a policy of force which cannot find a place in international law. As regards the notion of self-help, the Court is also unable to accept it: between independent States the respect for territorial sovereignty is an essential foundation for international relations.*[13]

As a subset of law regarding the use of force, the evolving norms and principles of the Cold War period appear to amount to a complete interdiction of acts of intervention. As one legal scholar put it after a lengthy discussion of possible exceptions to the principle of non-intervention (e.g., the support of self-determination and humanitarian intervention): 'In relation to unilateral action by states, there is no place in contemporary international law for a right of intervention.'[14]

This view would apply equally to the Soviet Union's normative justification of intervention in the socialist camp – the Brezhnev Doctrine. A major article in *Pravda* in 1968 noted that the Warsaw Pact action in Czechoslovakia had been criticised for violating principles of sovereignty and national self-determination. The commentator rejected this view, noting that the peoples of the socialist countries had every right to determine their countries' paths of development. However, 'any decision of theirs must damage neither socialism in their own country nor the fundamental interests of the other socialist countries'. If it did, it was the internationalist obligation of the USSR and other socialist states to act to reverse the process.[15] This rather transparently self-interested justification for the use of force to maintain a sphere of influence was roundly rejected not only outside the socialist camp, but also by some socialist countries (e.g., China and Yugoslavia).

The one apparent exception to the principle of non-intervention was assistance to incumbent regimes. If a state were sovereign and recognised as such by other states, and if the government of this state requested the assistance of another state to address an internal threat, such assistance would arguably be legal. For example, 'the sending of American forces to Lebanon and of British forces to Jordan (1958) was not regarded as contrary to international law and the United Nations Charter because it occurred upon the request of the "legal governments" '.[16] This view is, however, contested by some international lawyers, who suggest that the argument that 'consent legitimates what would otherwise be illegitimate' is spurious since recognition is inherently subjective. States are free to recognise whomever they want as the 'government'. Moreover, outside intervention on either side of a civil conflict would affect the outcome, thereby eroding the right of self-determination.[17] The logic here is attractive. However, one cannot say that this view represents a normative or legal consensus among states as most of them would accept that one element of sovereignty is the right to request external assistance.

In summary, the evolving Cold War normative framework regarding intervention was curiously contradictory: 'International law has developed a body of rules on human rights, which forbids states to ill-treat individuals, including their own nationals, but at the same time it has developed a body of rules restricting the (previously almost unlimited) right of states to use force.'[18] The normative basis justifying intervention widened but intervention in pursuit of these principles (and against established regimes) became increasingly illegitimate. In contrast, intervention in favour of governments, whatever their performance regarding human rights, remained permissible. In this respect, the normative evolution was profoundly conservative and hostile to the pursuit of the liberal agenda of human rights. The ideological bifurcation of the period further impeded the effort to insert human rights into international society's consideration of intervention.

The Cold War practice of intervention

Examination of the normative evolution during the Cold War is essential in understanding the role of intervention in the international system after the end of that period. However, these normative principles had little to do with the reality of state practice, which was informed by unilateral and egoistic conceptions of state interest in a profoundly competitive system dominated by power and ideology.[19] The discussion of the practice of intervention in this period can be divided into three parts: that of the superpowers and great powers, which was influenced by structural and global considerations; that of regional powers, which responded to more local political issues; and, finally, the limited experience of intervention by multilateral organisations.

The history of the Cold War is littered with episodes of intervention by the United States and the USSR in the internal affairs of other states, sometimes directly (as with the American intervention in the civil war in Vietnam, the Dominican Republic, Grenada and Panama or that of the USSR in Hungary, Czechoslovakia and Afghanistan) and sometimes indirectly (the use of allied or dependent states, such as Cuba in Angola and Ethiopia or the French/Belgian interventions in Shaba in 1977–78). These interventions were the local reflection of global bipolar competition. As a result of the constraints on war operating at the core of the international system, the expression of the superpowers' global and systemic conflict was largely transferred to the periphery. Here the constraints were less strong and the risks less imposing. The issues at stake were principally those of credibility and prestige rather than questions of vital strategic interest. The danger of intervention in each other's acknowledged spheres of interest was reduced by mutual recognition. Hence, the United States and its allies, although protesting loudly, did nothing to oppose the Soviet interventions in Hungary in 1956 and Czechoslovakia in 1968. The USSR behaved similarly with regard to American intervention in the Dominican Republic in 1965 and in Grenada in 1983.

It is unnecessary to discuss in detail the principal cases of direct and proxy superpower intervention during the Cold War. The key point is that their interventions were motivated by political and self-interested considerations. Intervention was not a matter of managing or resolving conflicts, defending human rights, or relieving human suffering. The aim was relative gain in the global bipolar struggle through the exercise of power in local conflicts and the internal affairs of target states, or the prevention of such gain by the other pole. There was, of course, a frequent ideological component (the promotion of democracy or of national liberation and socialist orientation), but these objectives were mixed in with the pursuit of strategic and geopolitical considerations. The ideological agendas of the superpowers were specific to them and did not reflect normative consensus in international society.

Moreover, the subordination of ideological and normative considerations to strategic factors was evident in cases where these were in contradiction to each other. It is hard to square US support for Mobutu Sese Seko in Zaire and Anastasio Somoza in Nicaragua or its assistance to the Chilean military in its overthrow of the democratically elected President of Chile with the liberal normative commitments of successive American governments. Likewise, the USSR's backing of allies in the Middle East, such as Gamal Abdel Nasser, Anwar Sadat (for a time) and Hafez al-Assad had little to do with the promotion of socialism. In a number of these cases, the beneficiaries of Soviet support ruthlessly suppressed indigenous communist and socialist movements. Interest and the quest for influence rather consistently carried the day over principle.

The superpowers were not the only ones to intervene in the internal affairs of states during the Cold War. The role of 'proxies' in the Soviet approach to the Third World has already been noted. Cuban interventions in Africa and Central America for the most part supported governments considered progressive and socialist in orientation. Although these interventions had an important ideological dimension, it is also worth noting that – given Cuba's substantial economic dependence on the USSR – Castro had an interest in underlining Cuba's utility in Soviet foreign policy. Elsewhere, the Warsaw Pact countries (with the exception of Romania) played an important role in support of Soviet intervention in Czechoslovakia as allies with an interest in the stability of the socialist system.

In the West, France and Great Britain also had a diverse

history of intervention during the Cold War. Their interventionism had several dimensions. In the first place, British and French intervention played a part in the Cold War. In several instances, this involved close political and logistical cooperation with the United States. British intervention in Jordan in 1958 was an element of a larger Anglo–American strategy designed to stabilise the conservative regimes of the Middle East in the face of Arab nationalism following the fall of Nuri Said in Iraq. The Franco–Belgian intervention in Shaba in 1978 occurred in close cooperation with the United States, which was seeking to brake the expansion of what Washington perceived to be a Soviet–Cuban sphere of influence in southern Africa. Although France had many reasons of its own for intervention in Africa, France and the United States shared the objective of containing communism.[20]

However, intervention by the European great powers during the Cold War cannot be fully explained in terms of bipolarity, since it was also a part of a sometimes less than enthusiastic, and often messy, process of decolonisation and the effort to redefine metropolitan relations with former colonies. In these respects, it frequently proceeded independently of, and sometimes in opposition to, American policy. The Anglo–French intervention in Egypt was in part a response to Nasser's challenge to British influence in the Middle East and to Nasser's support of the Front de Libération Nationale in Algeria. The Suez action managed to produce one of the few moments of agreement between the US and the USSR on an important question of international relations during the high Cold War. American hostility to the intervention, expressed, for example, in an unwillingness to assist the British in staving off a run on sterling, forced a British and French retreat.

Furthermore, in the post-colonial context, both former colonial powers intervened on occasion in support of the governments of their ex-colonies. After an early intervention in Tanganyika in 1964 to support the government of Julius Nyerere against a military mutiny, the British displayed increasing reluctance to engage in such activity, with the prominent exception of Oman, where British forces assisted the Sultan in putting down a prolonged revolt in the western part of the country that was supported by South Yemen and, indirectly, by the socialist bloc.

In contrast, in the context of its post-colonial bilateral defence cooperation and military assistance agreements, France frequently intervened in Francophone Africa to support friendly governments against internal (examples include the Cameroons, Congo-Brazzaville, Gabon, Niger, Mauritania and Rwanda) and external (the action against Polisario in Mauritania in 1977, in southern Zaire against the Front de Libération Nationale du Congo and in Chad against Libya in 1978–79) threats in the effort to sustain a French sphere of influence in the region.[21] In addition, on rare occasions the French acted to overthrow governments that had come to be seen as liabilities, as in 1979, when the French unseated Emperor Bokassa in the Central African Republic.[22]

Belgium, meanwhile, intervened immediately after independence in the Republic of Congo, ostensibly in an effort to defend its nationals and to restore order after a mutiny by the Congolese armed forces. Many suspected, however, that the real intention was to destabilise the Lumumba government and to retain privileged access to the country's economic resources. Since Belgium had acted without the consent of the authorities of the Republic of the Congo and against their wishes and its intrusion coincided with the effort of Katanga Province to secede, the intervention was widely condemned in the socialist and non-aligned blocs. Despite the Belgian claim to be acting on the basis of its right to defend its nationals, the UN Security Council called upon Belgium to withdraw its troops and authorised the Secretary-General to provide the Congolese authorities with military assistance to help the Congolese military and police to 'fulfil their tasks' (see below).[23]

From the perspective of this paper, what is important in the interventions of the colonial powers – like that of the United States and the USSR – is that the essence of intervention was egoistic and a reflection of their perceived interests. Normative issues had little impact on their conduct.

The third category of Cold War-era intervention was that conducted by regional powers, as with Egypt in Yemen in 1962, India in Bangladesh in 1971, South Africa in its neighbours' affairs in the 1970s and 1980s, Vietnam in Cambodia in 1978 and Tanzania in Uganda in 1979. In these cases, too, intervention had an essential political dimension. In the case of Yemen, Egypt intervened in response to an invitation by the new nationalist regime in North Yemen, which was facing a challenge from the royalist opposition supported by Saudi Arabia. The case was one episode in the longer and broader struggle between radical Arab nationalism and the traditionalist regimes of the region.[24] India, meanwhile, intervened in the civil war in East Pakistan not only to stop the flow of refugees, but also to take advantage of the situation to dismember its regional rival.[25] South Africa's interventionist activities reflected the desire not only to target the African National Congress, the Pan-Africanist Congress and the Southwest Africa People's Organisation (SWAPO), but also to destabilise, if not to overthrow, the regimes of socialist orientation in the region that were supporting the anti-apartheid movement and facilitating a perceived spread of Soviet and Cuban influence in southern Africa.

Several of these interventions, and notably those of India in Bangladesh, Tanzania in Uganda in 1979 and Vietnam in Cambodia in 1978, had a humanitarian dimension.[26] The Pakistani army's violence against the Bengali population of East Pakistan is considered to be one of the principal cases of genocide in the twentieth century.[27] The Indian invasion ended these massacres. Vietnamese action against the Khmer Rouge halted Cambodia's auto-genocide. And the overthrow of Idi Amin by Tanzanian forces removed a regime that had been responsible for between 100,000 and 500,000 murders.[28] In this sense, one might say that these interventions were humanitarian in their consequences.

But in all three cases, the intervening governments acted subsequent to attacks on their territory, and justified their actions not with regard to humanitarian or human rights norms, but by reference to the right of self-defence in international law. Moreover, in the Security Council debates on Vietnam's intrusion into Cambodia, several council members questioned whether the action could be justified on humanitarian grounds. The four NATO members of the council that participated in the debate took the position that even grave violations of human rights could not justify military intervention. The French representative provided a paradigmatic version of the pluralist conception of international society, reminiscent in a way of Castlereagh's reaction to proposed humanitarian intervention in Greece (see above), asserting that the idea that intervention could be justified because a regime was detestable was extremely dangerous and could compromise both order and law in the international system.[29] The judgement of the United Nations in this instance was evident in the organisation's refusal to seat the new, Vietnamese-imposed government. Instead, Khmer Rouge diplomats continued to represent the country.

The fourth category of intervention in the Cold War was that of multilateral organisations. In general, bipolarity and the global rivalry of the two superpowers strongly limited the interventionist role of the United Nations. There is only one major example of intervention by the UN in a civil conflict during the period – that of ONUC in the Republic of Congo (Léopoldville) in July 1960 and lasting until 1964.[30] After the rapid post-independence failure of the Congolese state, a military mutiny and Belgian intervention, and in the context of a threat of competitive superpower engagement and a request from the Congolese government, the UN Security Council asked Belgium to withdraw its forces and dispatched a peacekeeping force. The deployment was based on consent; the mandate did not contemplate the use of force.

Despite the arrival of peacekeepers, the situation continued to degenerate, in part as a result of attempts by the province of Katanga to secede. In February 1961, the Security Council adopted a supplementary resolution on the crisis, which envisaged the use of force to prevent civil war. Subsequently, the United Nations became a participant in the civil war, with a mandate to secure the removal of foreign military and paramilitary forces, and in the context of a clear rejection of the Katangan claim to independence.

Several aspects of this evolution are important. The Congolese government consented. The principal objectives of the UN operation were peace, stability and the preservation of the territorial integrity of the republic both through resistance to the secession of Katanga and through the effort to ensure the removal of foreign mercenaries. UN intervention did not address the issue of relations between the state and its people; instead it sought to re-establish the state. Second, although the UN troops were authorised to use force, the relevant resolutions did not evoke those articles in the Charter (e.g., articles 39 and 42) that permitted intervention into areas of essentially domestic jurisdiction on the basis of an identified threat to international peace and security. The thrust of the key resolution (161 – February 1961) was the prevention of civil war, not the achievement of a political settlement. The US representative on the council specifically stated that the authorisation to use force was restricted by the Charter's prohibition on intervention in internal affairs. Although the mandates and actions of the force *de facto* favoured first the anti-Lumumba faction in the central government and then the central government over the rebels in Katanga, the Security Council specifically avoided any mention of the use of force to impose a settlement.[31] Indeed, the reluctance of ONUC to intervene forcefully in the conflict in Katanga created significant tension between the UN and the consenting government, leading to clashes between the national army and UN units in the field.

The experience in Congo highlighted the limits on the UN's capacity to intrude in the domestic affairs of states and the dangers for the organisation itself in attempting to do so.[32] It was also illustrative of the subtleties of international opinion regarding intervention and its relationship to sovereignty. The restricted quality of the mandate reflected the caution of the permanent members of the Security Council, rather than the views of the post-colonial states.[33] Although, in general, the Third World members of the organisation are perceived to be the principal constituency for non-intervention, in this instance the opposite was the case. Many Third World states who were participating in ONUC in fact withdrew from the force because it was not interventionist enough (i.e. the UN refused to use force against Katanga). This anomaly reflects the fact that a direct engagement in the political and military struggle on the side of the central government would have been directed at impeding secession and enhancing Congo's sovereignty.

The other multilateral interventions of the period involved regional organisations. The OAS sent a multilateral force to replace US units in the Dominican Republic in 1965. The regional debates surrounding the operation suggested a growing disillusionment with the hegemonic policy of the United States in the region, and the Dominican experience strongly reinforced regional norms of non-intervention. The USSR cloaked its intervention in Czechoslovakia under the Warsaw Pact, but here too the hegemonic quality of the intervention was unmistakable. The Organisation of Eastern Caribbean states requested and participated in the US intervention in Grenada, again adding a multilateral veneer to a basically unilateral action.

Elsewhere, the OAU made several efforts to intervene in the internal conflicts of member states, the most notable example being the deployment of the 'Neutral Force' in Chad in 1981.[34] This experience demonstrated the weakness of the organisation's capabilities in the area of conflict management. That this is the sole significant case of multilateral intervention by the OAU during the Cold War is a good illustration of member states' lack of enthusiasm for the development of such an instrument of regional security.

To summarise, the practice of intervention during the Cold War was largely unilateral, statist and motivated by the pursuit of power and other egoistic interests in an anarchical bipolar system. Multilateral organisations played a minor role in the practice of intervention but a more important one in the strengthening of norms of sovereignty and non-intervention. Although human rights questions took on a more prominent place in international law during this period, this had little effect on the politics of intervention, which was weakly constrained by normative considerations. Several interventions of the period had significant and positive humanitarian consequences. But these were incidental to the political logic underlying the operations.

Chapter 4

The Interlude of 'New Political Thinking'

The rise of new political thinking in the USSR towards the end of the Cold War dramatically altered the practice of superpower intervention. It appeared that the Soviet leaders had concluded that, in a period where they sought an improvement in their relations with the United States and Western European states, local wars and competitive intervention in the Third World were at best a distraction or, worse, an impediment to attaining their principal foreign policy objective. They therefore sought to remove this obstacle. The Soviet Union reduced and then ceased its support of the Ethiopian, Angolan, and Nicaraguan governments. It withdrew its forces from Afghanistan. It encouraged the Vietnamese to cooperate in the international settlement process in Cambodia. Its financial support of Cuban deployments of force in Africa and Central America also diminished, as did its general assistance to Cuba. This shift in Soviet policy pushed the Cubans towards a less ambitious foreign policy. The reduction in assistance to Vietnam had the same effect.

At the same time, Mikhail Gorbachev declared the supremacy of the 'common idea of humanity,' his desire for a 'de-ideologisation' of international relations and his country's support of a more proactive UN role in the effort to make and keep the peace.[1] These changes in the Soviet position – and the constructive response of George Bush's administration – sparked a long series of UN initiatives (supported by the US and the USSR) to resolve the Third World conflicts that had troubled Soviet–American relations and regional security over the previous decade. With the unanimous support of the Security Council, the UN assisted in the negotiation of the withdrawal of Soviet forces from Afghanistan in 1989 and Vietnamese forces from Cambodia in 1991–92. The UN provided a small observer force (UNGOMAP) in the former case to monitor Soviet withdrawal. In the latter, the Vietnamese were replaced by a substantial multifaceted UN presence (UNTAC) to assist in the process of political settlement, the organisation and holding of elections and the re-establishment of the country's administration.

Elsewhere, after a deal was brokered between South Africa and SWAPO in 1988, the UN deployed a substantial peace force and transitional authority (UNTAG) to manage that country's movement towards sovereign statehood. In addition, it deployed a peacekeeping force to Angola (UNAVEM) to assist in that country's (ultimately unsuccessful) transition to peace, while contributing substantially to the resolution of the civil war in Mozambique (UNMOZ). It appeared that competitive intervention had been replaced by an incipient Soviet–American condominium committed to the reinforcement of peace and security on the basis of common values. The coalition action in the Iraq–Kuwait conflict in 1990–91, meanwhile, raised the possibility of collective use of force to eliminate threats to peace and security.

Chapter 5

Post-Cold War Intervention

The disappearance of bipolarity greatly diminished the significance of local conflict in the strategic calculations of the great powers for a time. Although conflicts in immediate proximity to the borders of the West (e.g., Yugoslavia) or to those of the Russian successor to the USSR (e.g., the rash of civil conflicts along Russia's southern periphery) continued to draw their attention, as did those that plausibly threatened key resources (e.g., the Iraq–Kuwait war), the dynamic of bipolarity and global ideological struggle that occasioned the globalisation of great power intervention no longer operated. Moreover, with the passage of time the principal colonial powers had largely worked out their problems of disengagement and their strategic focus was increasingly Europe itself. Their engagement in the affairs of their former possessions declined accordingly. One might have anticipated in this context a reduction in the incidence of intervention.

There is, however, little evidence of a decline in interventionism in world politics. Instead, there appears to be a change in its form and content. The incidence of unilateral great power intervention dropped markedly, although examples remained: the United States intruding into Panama in 1989 to remove Manuel Noriega, and the Russian Federation interfering repeatedly in the affairs of post-Soviet neighbours such as Moldova, Georgia and Tajikistan.

Moreover, the UN Security Council, liberated from the structural contradiction among its permanent members and intoxicated by the cooperative euphoria of the Gorbachev era, became far more active in responding to threats to peace and security with mandates for keeping or enforcing peace. This increase in activity was accompanied by a considerable broadening of the parameters of the concept of 'threats to international peace and security' and a corresponding widening of the qualification of sovereignty in Article 2 (7) of the Charter.

These changes reflected not only the transformation in relations between the great powers but also the evolving nature of war. Interstate war had largely disappeared by the end of the Cold War, while the incidence of internal war continued to rise. Although strategic interest in such conflicts had perhaps diminished, engagement was difficult to avoid for other reasons closely linked to the character of these wars.[1] Although at the beginning of the twentieth century there were approximately eight times as many combatant deaths in war as non-combatant ones, by the end of the century the reverse was the case. The numbers of persons displaced by war had grown considerably. Whereas in 1975, there were approximately 2.4 million refugees world-wide, in 1995 there were estimated to be 14.5 million.[2] The numbers of persons internally displaced by war grew even more substantially:

> When internally displaced persons (IDPs) were first counted in 1982, 1.2 million were found in eleven countries. By 1997 the number had soared to more than 20 million in at least 35 countries.[3]

The explosion in civilian deaths and mass displacement was tied to the fact that the pursuit of civil war was widely spread across populated territories. Furthermore, in multi-ethnic societies at least, these wars involved not merely political and military groupings, but entire communities and their identities. The objectives of war frequently included not only the conquest of territory and/or control of government but also the destruction or the removal of the adversary population. In such conditions, the distinction between military and civilian was greatly weakened. The result was humanitarian crisis, if not genocide. The rapid rise in numbers of persons displaced within and between countries dramatically altered the interests of major states *vis-à-vis* internal conflicts. It raised the prospect of substantial movements of people across borders, overpowering existing border control and asylum procedures and creating substantial potential domestic political and economic costs.

Many of these phenomena were hardly new. But the globalisation of means of communication made it much more difficult to ignore the resulting human suffering. Citizens watched it on television, and their desire that something 'should be done' was unsurprising. The result in the developed states was strong pressure on governments from public opinion to assist and protect the victims of these catastrophes. States, intergovernmental organisations and non-governmental organisations were increasingly predisposed to deliver assistance and protection **within** zones of conflict, given the increasing reluctance of states to welcome asylum-seekers.[4]

In these conditions, there appeared to have been several significant changes in the place of intervention in world politics. Notably, great power unilateralism largely disappeared and multilateral organisations, acting on the basis of liberal norms and usually on the basis of legal authorisation, came to play an increasingly prominent interventionist role. These practices raised significant questions about the parameters of state sovereignty, domestic jurisdiction and the legitimate use of force. As with the previous chapter, this one begins with a review of normative developments and then turns to a consideration of practice in order to assess the significance of normative change.

Post-Cold War normative developments

The key normative challenge of the 1990s concerned the understanding of sovereignty. In January 1992, the Security Council members asked the new Secretary-General, Boutros Boutros-Ghali, to prepare 'an analysis and recommendations on ways of strengthening and making more efficient within the framework and provisions of the Charter the capacity of the United Nations for preventive diplomacy, for peacemaking and for peacekeeping'.[5]

In his response, Boutros-Ghali noted a number of profound changes in the international system, and notably the collapse of ideological barriers to collective action on security issues, the growing consensus of permanent members on issues before the Council, the retreat of authoritarianism in the face of a growing wave of democratisation, the peaceful liberation of the countries of Central and Eastern Europe, the globalisation of communications, and the increasingly central role of human rights issues in international relations and in the work of the United Nations and its agencies.

On the negative side, he stressed the deterioration in the security of many of the world's regions, the deepening economic problems of much of the South and the explosive growth in numbers of refugees and internally displaced persons. On this basis he concluded that there were strong reasons for abandoning the notion of 'absolute sovereignty' in the pursuit of common and universal values: 'The time of absolute and exclusive sovereignty ... has passed; its theory was never matched by reality'.[6] He affirmed that there was a growing sentiment in the international community that the conditions of the post-Cold War era provided an opportunity to realise the fundamental goals of the United Nations – justice, human rights, social progress and a larger liberty for all.

His relativistic conception of sovereignty reflected an increasingly widely held view in the North that the state's enjoyment of sovereign rights in international society should be linked to its fulfilment of responsibilities to its citizens. As Boutros-Ghali's successor, Kofi Annan, put it in 1998:

> *The Charter protects the sovereignty of peoples* (sic). *It was never meant as a license for governments to trample on human rights and human dignity. Sovereignty means responsibility, not just power.*[7]

In this view, the systematic violation of human rights could degrade the state's sovereignty and diminish the force of legal protections against intervention,[8] especially when such intervention occurred under the mandate of an organisation authorised to use force (the UN under Chapter VII of the Charter). This line of argument was particularly strong in France in the articulation of a duty to intervene (*devoir d'ingérence*) in humanitarian crises, which implied a right to act within the domestic jurisdiction of a state without its consent.[9]

But what was the legal basis of this right? As noted above, the only Charter exception to the prohibition of intervention appeared at the end of Article 2 (7), where it was noted that the proscription of intervention in domestic jurisdiction did not prejudice the application of Chapter VII, which established the rights and responsibilities of the Security Council in the face of threats to international peace and security. It was not surprising, in consequence, that the decade witnessed a substantial expansion in the interpretation of 'threats to international peace and security' in the effort to respond in an effective way to humanitarian problems within states affected by civil war.

The logic of this expansion in meaning was reasonably clear; a humanitarian crisis or the systematic violation of human (individual and/or group) rights in civil wars created externalities that affected the security of neighbouring states if not of entire regions. Waves of refugees could overcome the infrastructure of neighbouring host states and could destabilise their internal politics by altering ethnic balances. Turkey's unwillingness to accept large numbers of Kurdish refugees from Iraq in 1991 was tied, for example, to a continuing civil conflict with its own Kurdish population and its consequent unwillingness to accept an increase in the size of this minority in areas of the country that it already had difficulty in controlling.

Moreover, military forces retreating from one state could use their refuge in neighbouring territory to recover their strength and resume the struggle. This in turn could provoke military attack on the territory of the host state. Alternatively, a state affected by cross-border raiding by expelled combatants might seek to destabilise the neighbour harbouring such forces and tolerating their activities (see the discussion of Central Africa below). Likewise, conflicts in one country ran the risk of entangling related groups in neighbouring ones. For example, the conflict within Azerbaijan between Armenians and Azeris quickly resulted in intervention by Armenia in support of their fellow Armenians, and the occupation of some 15 per cent of Azerbaijan's territory. In Kashmir, continuing violence between some Muslim Kashmiris and the

Indian government resulted in the activation of an array of militant groups in neighbouring Pakistan to support the Kashmiri insurgents within India. Cross-border raiding, military and technical assistance, and terrorist attacks carried the risk of re-igniting the Indian–Pakistani conflict, this time in circumstances where both sides possessed nuclear weapons.

This sort of reasoning was evident in the resolutions of the council mandating international action in the face of civil war during the 1990s. Resolution 688 (1991) identified the repression of the civilian population of Iraq – and especially the campaign against the Kurds – as a threat to peace. It likewise defined the movement of Kurds towards Iraq's frontiers and cross-border military incursions as threats before demanding an end to Iraq's repression.[10]

In Somalia in 1991–92, Resolution 733 noted the implications of the military and humanitarian situation in that country for regional security and the concern of the council that it constituted a threat to regional peace and security. It requested that the Secretary-General undertake the necessary measures to assure the delivery of humanitarian assistance and invoked Chapter VII of the Charter to impose an embargo on arms imports to the country.[11] In the resolutions that followed (746, 751, 775),[12] the council repeated this concern over threats to regional security emanating from the civil conflict. In resolution 794, at the beginning of December 1992, the council determined that the Somali situation constituted a threat to peace and security, noted the remaining obstacles to the delivery of relief and the dangers to humanitarian personnel working in the country, and declared its determination to create an environment in which it was possible to mount humanitarian operations in security, as well as to restore stability and the authority of law. It went on to invoke Chapter VII to authorise a military operation led by the United States without the consent of Somalia.[13]

Later, in the case of Bosnia, the UN Security Council authorised the use of force to protect displaced persons and minority communities in security zones, to facilitate the delivery of humanitarian assistance and, later, conflict resolution under NATO auspices. Finally, the Security Council belatedly determined 'that the magnitude of the humanitarian crisis in Rwanda constitutes a threat to peace and security', and, acting under Chapter VII, mandated the deployment of a multinational force to protect affected civilians and to assist in the delivery of relief.[14]

In subsequent cases, this trend broadened to embrace the preservation or restoration of democratic rights and institutions. In Haiti (1994), the Security Council authorised *Operation Uphold Democracy* in the effort to re-establish the government of Bertrand Aristide.[15] In the face of this decision and impending American invasion, the *de facto* authorities in Port-au-Prince decided to resign and depart into exile. Similarly, in October 1997, the Security Council, acting under Chapter VII, authorised the intervention of ECOWAS to restore the democratic government and constitutional authority of Sierra Leone.[16]

This series of decisions might suggest that international society was coming to the acceptance of a norm legitimising multilateral intervention for the protection and promotion of human rights. At a more profound level, these developments perhaps represented a change in the balance between order and justice as objectives of international society in favour of the promotion of justice, and a consequent modification of the content of sovereignty. In extreme cases, such as Bosnia, Kosovo and East Timor, multilateral intervention culminated in the partial or complete suspension of the sovereign rights of states and the establishment of forms of international administration.[17] In short, it appeared that the liberal and solidarist agenda had carried the day over the pluralist conception of international society and its understanding of intervention. The normative gap between the principle of non-intervention and the protection of human rights appeared to be narrowing through a gradual redefinition of the parameters of sovereignty.[18]

But this conclusion is perhaps hasty. First, there was strong continuing resistance in international society to the erosion of the rights of states. This rearguard action is amply evident in the relevant council debates. In the Council's discussions on intervention in northern Iraq, a significant number of members (including China, Cuba, Yemen and Zimbabwe) expressed strong reservations about the implications of Resolution 688. India and China abstained from the vote for the same reasons. The resolutions themselves reflect this ambivalence. Resolution 688, for example, reaffirms the sovereignty of Iraq while it authorises intervention in its internal affairs. After the adoption of the resolution, and in view of Iraq's expressed opposition to the actions of Britain, France and the United States, the Secretariat made an intensive effort to obtain Iraqi consent to the international presence, and succeeded in obtaining the agreement of the Iraqi authorities to the presence of a small force of UN guards to reassure the returning Kurds. Finally, the significance of the case as a precedent is unclear, since Iraq was an aggressor that had recently been defeated by an international coalition operating under a Security Council mandate and was subject to international sanctions. The UN was already playing an important role within Iraq's domestic jurisdiction (namely, the effort to control Iraq's production of weapons of mass destruction through intrusive inspection by UNSCOM).

In the case of Somalia, China and Zimbabwe, among others, underlined the unique character of the situation in council debates. They did so to minimise the prospect that UN action there would constitute a precedent for subsequent action elsewhere. The resolutions themselves again stress the uniqueness of the circumstances. Among the case's peculiarities, moreover, was the absence of a recognised sovereign authority in the country. The importance of action without consent is unclear when there is no authority that can consent. Some authors also suggest that China failed to oppose the authorisation of armed intervention because it believed that the African group would do so. When the anticipated African resistance did not emerge, China was not in a position to oppose on its own.[19]

In Haiti, the debates and resolutions demonstrated the substantial resistance to the idea of multilateral intervention to promote democracy, not only from China but from an important group of Latin American states, including Brazil, Mexico, Cuba, Uruguay and Venezuela. The council once again emphasised the specificity of the situation. Judgement concerning the significance of this case is complicated by the fact that the government in exile, which was recognised as the legitimate authority, finally consented to the intervention.[20] Its consent was a *sine qua non* in the adoption of the resolution. And, of course, the *de facto* authorities also consented, although under duress.

The cases of Croatia and Bosnia were not, in a legal sense, interventions, since the two governments consented to the presence and role of foreign forces. The third case in former Yugoslavia – NATO intervention in Kosovo in 1999 – amply demonstrated the normative ambiguities surrounding the issue of humanitarian intervention. In this case, the NATO powers did not request a Security Council mandate, since they were reasonably certain that a resolution along such lines would be vetoed by Russia and/or China.[21] Without a Security Council mandate under Chapter VII, such action is arguably a violation of the United Nations Charter. As such, it is hard to see the action as evidence of an emerging international norm. On the other hand, when Russia submitted a resolution condemning NATO's action, it was resoundingly defeated in the council. Some have taken this to indicate backhanded UN endorsement of the operation.

The Charter is not the only authoritative indication of state obligation in cases of this type. States have obligations in international humanitarian law with respect to populations victimised in war or vulnerable to genocide independently of the Charter. Arguably, therefore, and when the council is unable to respond effectively to such situations as a result of the veto, intervention without Security Council authorisation is lawful. In this context, several members of the council maintained that, even if an action contravened the Charter, it was legal because it conformed to general international law (overwhelming humanitarian necessity).[22] Others (for example, the International Commission on Kosovo) suggested that NATO's action, while illegal, was legitimate.[23]

Many states, however, greeted the Kosovo action with outrage. The non-aligned movement responded by declaring that 'we reject the so-called "right of humanitarian intervention" which has no legal basis in the UN Charter or in general principles of international law'.[24] Reflecting Russia's sensitivity not just about Kosovo but also regarding Chechnya, the Russian President Vladimir Putin, in one of his first substantial statements on foreign policy, noted that humanitarian intervention could not be a basis

for overriding 'such basic principles of international law as sovereignty and territorial integrity'.[25] Later, in the bilateral statement at
the moment of signature of their countries' Treaty of Friendship
and Cooperation, the heads of state of Russia and China asserted
that:

> *The formation of a fair and rational new international order
> is coming up against a number of challenges. Russia and
> China will be making joint efforts for strengthening the
> leading role of the UN and its Security Council in world
> affairs and for countering any attempts to subvert the
> fundamental norms of international law with the help of
> such concepts as 'humanitarian intervention' and 'limited
> sovereignty'.*[26]

More broadly, Vladimir Baranovsky noted a pervasive hostility
towards the concept of humanitarian intervention amongst the
Russian international relations and foreign policy communities,
which considered it internally inconsistent, lacking in clear criteria,
dangerous in its practical implications not least for the territorial
integrity of states (e.g., Kosovo), susceptible to double standards, a
cover for political agendas of one sort or another, a potentially
open-ended invitation to aggressive behaviour in international
relations, and, for these reasons, corrosive of international order.[27]

For both Russia and China, hostility to this form of intervention presumably reflected political vulnerabilities and the possibility that they might be targets if such a principle were established.
Both Russia's wars in Chechnya raised serious human rights issues. In returning to war in 1999, moreover, Russia appeared to
breach a number of the Russian Federation's specific treaty and
political obligations.[28] The possibility that external forces might
take advantage of the war to embarrass and isolate Russia was
evident in the discussion of the issue in the Parliamentary
Assembly of the Council of Europe (CoE) in 1999–2000, and the
suspension of Russian voting rights in that body. The establishment of a norm of humanitarian intervention might have affected
Russian interests not only with regard to its own domestic jurisdiction but also in the sphere of influence it claimed, the CIS. Russian
policy in the former Soviet Union had long displayed sensitivity to

the intrusion of foreign military forces into this space (see below). Russia was unlikely to be enthusiastic about new justifications for such intrusion. China, meanwhile, had long faced and strongly resisted external criticism of its human rights record. Its low-intensity war against Uighur insurgents in Xinjiang displayed little sensitivity to the rights of this minority population.

However, the problem here was not merely one of specific political interests. Both Russia and China expressed serious questions about the universality of the norms informing the use of force to promote rights within other states. Many in both countries took the view that the agenda here was hegemonic – to impose Western principles on non-Western states. In short, both Russia and China had general and specific political reasons for resisting the emergence of a new solidarist norm of humanitarian intervention. Russian and Chinese scepticism regarding humanitarian intervention in general was even stronger when the possibility of such action without UN Security Council mandates was considered.[29]

This political basis for Russian and Chinese resistance to the notion of normatively based intervention for the most part applied to many of the members of the non-aligned movement and regional organisations such as ASEAN, too.[30] They faced serious problems sustaining domestic jurisdiction and territorial integrity in the face of minority challenges from below. Many of the regimes governing these states, moreover, were unrepresentative and were threatened to some degree by democratic movements. Their effort to cope with such challenges frequently involved systematic violation of the rights of ethnic and political groups within their borders. The establishment of norms regarding rights-based intervention potentially, if not actually, threatened their hold on power. Moreover, they resided in often unsettled regions, and often faced longstanding adversaries. They, too, feared that such norms might be manipulated by hostile states to justify action against them.

Finally, in the case of East Timor, it was difficult to see exactly what relevance UN-mandated intervention has to a general consideration of the possibility of an emerging solidarist consensus on intervention, since the United Nations had never recognised Indonesian annexation of the territory after Portuguese withdrawal. The case would appear to pertain more to established norms concerning post-colonial self-determination than to the matter of humanitarian intervention.

In summary, the movement of international society towards acceptance of liberal and solidarist norms of intervention was not clear. Firstly, the consent of states remained extremely important in the deliberations and decisions of the Security Council, which drew into question the extent of the erosion of sovereignty.[31] Secondly, the council habitually emphasised the uniqueness of the circumstances in which it decided to mandate intervention, and, consequently, highlighted the exceptional character of those interventions that it supported.[32] Thirdly, the debates of the council, wider commentaries and the reactions of numerous states suggested that this normative evolution was stronger amongst the Western states than elsewhere. The liberal agenda was resisted by a coalition that included Russia, China and the bulk of the states of the South. Although the normative dimension of intervention was considerably more important in the 1990s than previously, these norms were not universally accepted and were sometimes actively opposed. The evident decline in cooperation amongst the five permanent members of the Security Council prior to the events of 11 September 2001 suggested that the consensus necessary to the definition of threats to peace and security and, thereby, to override domestic jurisdiction on liberal grounds was increasingly difficult to sustain. In short, there were numerous substantial reasons to doubt the emergence of a liberal norm of multilateral intervention after the Cold War.[33]

Moreover, it was possible to perceive this proposed normative evolution as a reflection of unipolarity and Western hegemony. Advocacy of this right was particularly strong at the core of the international system, in Western Europe and North America. The norm appeared to pertain to core relations with the periphery. That periphery contested the universality of the norm. If propositions concerning the legitimacy of humanitarian intervention were an ideological manifestation of power-political domination, then one might have expected that, in the longer term and in the face of probable Russian recovery and the economic and military growth of China and India, the dilution of power-political hegemony would also reduce the impact of Western and American ideological and normative hegemony.

The post-Cold War practice of intervention

The practice of intervention in the post-Cold War period was dominated at the global level by actions mounted by coalitions of the willing under UN mandates (UNITAF in Somalia in late 1992, Operation Uphold Democracy in Haiti in 1994, NATO's insertion of IFOR into Bosnia-Herzegovina in 1995, the Italian-led Operation Alba in Albania in 1997 and the Australian-led INTERFET in East Timor in 1999) or by particular states with similar mandates (e.g., France's *Opération Turquoise* in Rwanda in mid-1994). In some instances, regional organisations played an essential (NATO in Bosnia) or significant (the OAS in Haiti, the OSCE in Bosnia) role as the UN's agents of choice in dealing with specific aspects of the crisis in question. In other cases, the organisations operated independently of the UN (e.g., the intervention of ECOWAS in Liberia and Sierra Leone, the CIS in Georgia and Tajikistan, and NATO in the Federal Republic of Yugoslavia). However, for the most part, regional operations were authorised or approved by the UN Security Council, either prospectively (NATO in Bosnia), or retrospectively (ECOWAS in Liberia and Sierra Leone, the CIS in Georgia and Tajikistan).[34] The great exception (in terms of the lack of a UNSC mandate) was NATO in Kosovo.

From a chronological point of view, there is a reasonably clear-cut period of multilateral interventionism in the 1990s. Perhaps in reaction to the apparent success in resolving a number of prolonged local conflicts towards the end of the Cold War and the rebuff of Iraqi aggression in 1990–91 and taking into account the appearance of a number of post-Cold War conflicts in Europe, there was initially a rapid increase in the number of interventions and of peace-support operations at the beginning of the decade. This died quickly. The debacle in Somalia in 1993 considerably deflated American enthusiasm for participation in peace enforcement and, more broadly, for 'assertive multilateralism'.

The new American caution was reflected in the stringent conditions on participation included in Presidential Decision Directive 25 (PDD-25), issued in the spring of 1994, just as the

Rwandan crisis broke out. As Weiss and Collins note, 'the United States would not become involved unless American interests could be advanced at acceptable risk; and at least seventeen conditions had to be fulfilled to indicate an acceptable risk'.[35] In the prevailing circumstances, the United States government strongly resisted the idea of multilateral peace enforcement in Rwanda, greatly reducing the prospect for an effective international response. The paucity of media presence on the ground reduced the degree of domestic pressure on them to act. The frustrations of the UN, the EU, the OSCE and NATO in the former Yugoslavia contributed to the reversal in the mood of the international community. UN action was also increasingly constrained by its financial crisis, which was due in large part to the refusal of the United States to pay its accumulated and delinquent contributions to the general and peacekeeping budgets.[36]

In consequence, the number of peacekeeping or peace-enforcement missions declined markedly from 1994 to 1997. The role of UN forces in such operations diminished even more rapidly, with regional organisations (for example, NATO and ECOWAS) taking the initiative. The end of the decade, however, witnessed the return of the UN to a more active position in the effort to resolve conflicts such as the civil war in Sierra Leone, East Timor, and (potentially) the Democratic Republic of Congo.

The periodicity of multilateral intervention drew the establishment of a solidarist norm of intervention into question. So, too, did the lack of specificity in the norm itself. The idea that the international community had a right to intervene in response to particularly bad violations of the rights of the citizens of a country seemed plausible. But it was not clear where the threshold is beyond which such intervention is legitimate. A second problem concerned what rights were to be included in the justification of intervention. Intervention to prevent or to end systematic violation of basic rights of citizens (e.g., survival) seemed to enjoy greater acceptance than that to end a denial of political rights, such as the right to freedom of association and exercise of franchise. A third problem (in the light of the above discussion of Kosovo) concerned whether the right pertained in general (that is to say, to all states) or whether it required authoritative determination (through the

Security Council). It was difficult to see how the norm could possess significant causal weight unless these questions were clearly answered.

The embeddedness of the norm was also drawn into question by the selectivity of international response to humanitarian crises. If the practice of intervention was guided by an evolving regime of universal norms, then one might have expected it to be universal in application. But it was not. The list of failed states where the state did not provide meaningful protection and the rights of populations were more or less systematically violated by the state, and where there was no international reaction compatible with the liberal normative position, was long. Sudan was an eloquent example. The latest stage of that country's civil war began in the early 1980s. Several hundred thousand civilians died, many of them as a result of the punitive actions of their own government, and others as a result of that government's incapacity to exercise effective jurisdiction over a substantial portion of its territory. The violence produced millions of displaced persons. It also generated cross-border spill-over effects to the detriment of security and peace in the broader neighbourhood. The international community avoided coercive engagement, watching from the wings.

The 1994 genocide in Rwanda was another example. In this case, the UN did insert a peacekeeping force (UNAMIR) in 1993 to facilitate the process of political settlement of that country's long civil war, and with the consent of both parties. Several months later, in January 1994, the commander of the UN force warned the Secretariat of the possibility of genocide. Personnel of the Department of Peacekeeping Operations read the telex but apparently did not show it either to the Secretary-General[37] or to Security Council members. UNDPKO refused to recommend an expansion of the UNAMIR mandate that might have prevented or mitigated the crisis.

In April 1994, when the genocide began, and in the face of the murder of several Belgian peacekeepers, the council decided to reduce rather than to expand the force. Several members suggested the complete removal of UNAMIR. There was no willingness in the council to enlarge the mandate or the force in order to address the crisis effectively. For several weeks, the council refused to identify the crisis as genocide in order to avoid obligations under the Convention against genocide.[38]

It was only on 17 May that the council reversed its position on UNAMIR, expanding the latter's mandate to include the protection of civilians and security and support for the delivery of humanitarian relief.[39] A month later the council (acting under Chapter VII) authorised the deployment of a multinational force to hold the line while the expansion of UNAMIR proceeded.[40] This led to the dispatch of *Opération Turquoise*, in which French units occupied the south-west of the country in order to protect civilians threatened by the civil war. They were deployed in July, well after the climax of the atrocities. Some 800,000 civilians died. A million more were displaced.

The contrast between the international reaction to the crisis in Kosovo and the absence of reaction to the war in Chechnya provided yet another powerful example of the problem of selectivity in multilateral intervention on humanitarian grounds. The humanitarian consequences of the latter were considerably greater than those of the Serbs' actions in Kosovo prior to the NATO campaign. The selectivity of multilateral responses to humanitarian crises resulting from war drew into question the legitimacy of the 'new interventionism'.

This selectivity may be explained in large part by the interweaving of the normative agenda with considerations of state interest. With the exception of Somalia, intervention occurred where the intervening states perceived political interests that might be furthered through military action of this type. In northern Iraq, the trilateral UK–French–US intervention was strongly influenced by the fact that the country of destination for a considerable number of the displaced was Turkey, a NATO member and close ally. As noted earlier, Turkey already faced a revolt among its own Kurdish population. In such circumstances, Turkey was unwilling to accept several hundred thousand more Kurds flowing into a region that it was already having difficulty in controlling. The attention that the Yugoslav conflicts received reflected the problems that these conflicts raised for the European great powers and notably forced migration. Moreover, the continuation of Serb resistance to the preferences of the Western European powers risked drawing into question the credibility, if not the survival, of NATO. The invasion of Haiti was in part a response to the flood of Haitian migrants seeking refuge in Florida, the importance of that state in the American electoral process the United States, the influence of the Black Caucus in Congress and the significance of the black vote in the electoral base of President Clinton. French intervention in Rwanda reflected in the first place the geostrategic sense that France was losing out to the 'Anglo-Saxon' countries in Central Africa. Moreover, the French president acted on the basis of the judgement that intervention would play well in French domestic politics:

> *Once more the Socialists would appear to have 'le monopole du Coeur' (monopoly of the heart), something which always vastly irritated Conservative politicians, who were keen not to be seen as cold-blooded financiers and technocrats. In other words, Rwanda and its chopped-up babies now looked as if they could give good political mileage in terms of public opinion ratings.*[41]

In the case of East Timor, Australia's interest in regional stability, and strong pressure from civil society underpinned the state's willingness to play a leading role in this multilateral intervention. In general, intervention did not occur where such interests were weak or absent or when political interest militated against intrusion. Even the case of Somalia demonstrated the significance of perceived national interest in a backhanded way. The rapidity of the international community's retreat from Somalia highlights the fragility of international engagement when no significant perceived interests are at stake.

Considerations of national interest explain not only the actions of those who intervene, but also of those who did not oppose it. For example, given the attitude of India and China to interference in domestic jurisdiction, one might have expected stronger opposition from them to the actions in Iraq in 1991. This did not emerge. Their acquiescence may be explained in considerable measure by the particular circumstances of the period. India was negotiating several economic agreements with the United States and the Indian government did not wish to complicate that process.

The Chinese were seeking to break out of the isolation brought about by the events in Tienanmen Square in 1989. They did not wish to derail their gradual return to international respectability.

The Haitian case provided another example. One might have expected stronger Russian resistance to intervention in support of democracy, for reasons discussed above. However, at the time Russia was seeking authorisation for and financial assistance in its intervention in Georgia. The result was an informal trilateral accord between the US, Russia and France. The US and France would not oppose Russia's resolution on Georgia, and Russia would not oppose resolutions concerning intervention in Haiti and Rwanda. In the case of intervention to restore constitutional order in Sierra Leone, the lack of Chinese and Russian opposition may perhaps be explained by African support for the action and the Russian and Chinese unwillingness to run against a regional consensus in a matter where their interests were not at stake.

In summary, although there was evidence to suggest the growing influence of a liberal solidarist logic in multilateral decisions to intervene, it would have been premature to suggest that normative considerations had replaced those of political interest in decision-making on intervention. Solidarist and pluralist perspectives coexisted uneasily in this realm.

One other element of multilateral intervention deserves mention. Just as great power intervention during the Cold War tended to be concentrated in contested zones on the periphery of the central blocs, so in the 1990s multilateral intervention concentrated in areas outside the Western core. In this respect, one might argue that, in the largest sense, multilateral intervention had replaced the unilateral variant as a means whereby the great powers attempted to manage their interests in other areas. Although this suggests a degree of continuity between the two periods, it is important to note that the character of those interests had evolved. The strong link between intervention and bipolar competition in Cold War competition had disappeared. The interests to which the great powers responded in the post-Cold War period were far more fluid, tending to cluster around the externalities created by local crisis, in terms of either threats to specific interests (e.g., energy security, alliance credibility) or the pressure of public opinion generated by human suffering in civil war. There was no overarching strategic logic.

Moreover, although one of the principal motifs of intervention in the post-Cold War era was multilateralism, unilateral intervention had not disappeared, a matter largely ignored in the liberal enthusiasm for the rule-governed use of force to affect the internal arrangements of states. Patterns of unilateral intervention appeared to cluster in four areas. The first, and perhaps best known, was the series of Yugoslav interventions in support of Serb minorities in the new successor states of Croatia and Bosnia-Herzegovina. The Yugoslav Army actively supported Serb movements in creating independent structures of power in Eastern Slavonia and Krajina in Croatia and in eastern and northern Bosnia. The goals of the Milosevic regime were reasonably transparent. It was initially opposed to the break-up of the Federation, and subsequently sought to build a Greater Serbia that would take in territories in neighbouring republics populated or claimed by Serbs and to remove non-Serb populations from those areas. In this sense the apparently humanitarian interventions of the West and the United Nations in the former Yugoslavia were in considerable measure the reflection of prior political and military interventions by the Serbian authorities of the Federal Republic of Yugoslavia.

A second cluster occurred in the former USSR, in the form of Russian intervention in the Transdnestr conflict in Moldova, the South Ossetia and Abkhaz conflicts in Georgia and the civil war in Tajikistan.[42] In each of the three cases, Russian policy was complicated (or facilitated) by the presence of Russian forces stationed in theatre, a consequence of pre-collapse Soviet deployment patterns. Moldova hosted the Russian 14th Army, a formation that was very well equipped, since it had been designated as an echeloned unit to follow up on Warsaw Pact offensives to the west. It was located in an area with a substantial Russian and Ukrainian population and a valuable military–industrial base (Transdnestr Republic – TDR) that, in the aftermath of independence, sought to secede from Moldova.[43] Local separatist forces quickly confiscated considerable numbers of weapons from 14th Army stocks. That they could do so reflected the undermanning of the local Russian force, but also, plausibly, the sympathy of Russian officers for the community in which they lived, as well as, possibly, the sympathy of conservative forces in Moscow (e.g., Liberal Democratic Party of Russia and communist members of the Duma) for the dismemberment of Moldova. During the ensuing war in 1992, Russian officers were seconded or seconded themselves to TDR units to assist them in establishing control of their enclave.

In mid-1992, however, the Russian Defence Ministry sent General Alexander Lebed to restore control over the force. Open support of the secessionists ceased and a degree of discipline was restored. Later in the year, after a ceasefire mediated by Boris Yeltsin, Russia sent approximately 2,000 peacekeepers to the country. For the rest of the Yeltsin period, however, Russia made little effort to produce a durable agreement between the parties. This suggested that the Russian government had concluded that a durable political settlement would have contravened the Russian desire to sustain a degree of influence in this strategically significant region of the former Soviet Union.

The second major venue of post-Soviet Russian intervention was in Georgia. Here, civil conflict broke out over identity issues in the autonomous region of South Ossetia (SOAO) in 1989–1990. [44] Volunteers from the Russian Federation's Republic of North Ossetia were heavily involved in support of their ethnic kin in Georgia. Russia failed to close its border in order to prevent this intrusion. The unit of the Russian Ministry of Internal Affairs (MVD) stationed in South Ossetia's capital reportedly provided military assistance to the insurgents. When they left, some of their equipment remained in the hands of the *de facto* authorities in South Ossetia, enhancing their military capability. In mid-1992, Boris Yeltsin brokered a ceasefire between the Georgian and South Osset leaderships, and organised a peacekeeping force (made up of Russian, Georgian and Osset units) to police it. For several years, Russia attempted to establish and maintain close control over the process of political settlement. Once again, little progress was made towards a political resolution of the dispute. This reflected not only the intransigence of the parties, but also Russia's apparent lack of enthusiasm for the promotion of stability (and the reduction of Russian leverage) in its southern neighbour.

Subsequently, conflict broke out in the Abkhaz Autonomous Republic in Georgia in August 1992. Russia began the process of mediation sooner, with a number of ceasefire initiatives in early and mid-1993. These failed, in part as a result of the intervention of Russian forces stationed in Abkhazia and of Cossack and Chechen citizens of the Russian Federation on the side of the Abkhaz *de facto* authorities, which altered the military balance. Once again, the Russian authorities made no obvious effort to prevent the movement of armed Russian citizens across the border to assist the Abkhaz. Russian monitoring of the last war-time cease-fire (July 1993) was biased; the Georgians withdrew weapons from the region while the Abkhaz resupplied. This set the stage for the final phase of the war, in which the Georgian military and Georgian civilians were driven from the Abkhaz portion of Georgia.

At this stage, Georgia, faced with two insurgent regions and another rebellion in areas of Mingrelia adjacent to Abkhazia, was driven to the point of requesting military assistance from the Russian Federation. Georgia joined the CIS in October 1993. This was followed by a deployment of Russian marines that put down the rebellion in Mingrelia, and, later, by the informal deployment of an interposition force along the line of contact between Georgian and Abkhaz forces. This deployment formally became multilateral in May 1994, when the CIS authorised a peacekeeping force. However, the troop complement was, and remains, exclusively Russian, although Russian forces in theatre have been joined by a UN observer force (UNOMIG).

In the meantime, the United Nations sponsored a peace process that has continued to stumble along eight years later at the time of writing.[45] In the latest phase, Russia was holding up the adoption of a constitutional framework proposal by the Group of Friends of the Secretary-General to which the other 'friends' had agreed.[46] Although there were a number of points on which the Russians took issue with Abkhaz positions in negotiations, on balance their participation favoured the insurgent side and did not contribute positively to the quest for a final settlement.[47]

The third major example of regional intervention in the CIS is that of Russia (and the CIS) in Tajikistan from 1992 to the time of writing. The Tajik conflict – involving a democratic and Islamic challenge to the dominance of the former communist leadership, but reflecting also deep regional rivalries – was the most substantial post-Soviet conflict in terms of the numbers of casualties (civilian and military), the size of Russian intervention (which peaked at around 25,000 army and border troops) and the duration of hostilities (1992–97). Russia became involved, first unilaterally in the pro-government activities of the 201st Motor Rifle Division stationed in Dushanbe, and then multilaterally with the formation of a CIS force in 1993.[48] Russia's engagement, strongly encouraged by other regional states such as Uzbekistan, reflected concern over the spread of political Islam in post-Soviet Central Asia, as well as a more pragmatic desire to control the movement of contraband and people across the border between Afghanistan and Central Asia.[49] Russian intervention stabilised the government of Imomali Rakhmonov, and, unlike in other cases, the Russians successfully pressured the authorities into a political settlement involving a degree of power-sharing in 1997.[50] Russian forces remained in place, however, both for border control and for monitoring compliance with the agreement.

The interventions of Russia in the other former Soviet states were revealing in a number of ways. Firstly, to the extent that they were conscious acts of policy, they were motivated by classic power-political considerations: the maintenance of control over a sphere of influence and defence against potential threats from neighbouring areas. These external concerns were complemented by domestic political ones – the existence of strong lobbies in Russia that criticised Yeltsin and his colleagues for their abandonment of Russia's position in the region as a whole. If the government could be seen to be active in reasserting Russian influence in the 'near abroad', such criticism could be deflected.

Secondly, for much of the period in question Russia asserted special rights and responsibilities in the region that derogated the sovereign rights of its neighbours.[51] In essence, it claimed a *droit de regard* in the former Soviet Union similar to that embodied in America's Monroe Doctrine.[52] Intervention was one means of attaining this objective. Russian spokesmen did provide some normative justification for the enterprise, but this focused on order and stability, not sovereignty and equality or human rights. And the emphasis on order and stability reflected a concrete under-standing of specific national interests.

After 1992, Russian interventionism in the former Soviet Union was placed in the nascent multilateral context of the CIS. This reflected a concern to legitimise the use of force in local conflicts both regionally and internationally. In the realm of secur-ity, however, Russia sought to use the institution hegemonically as an instrument of control. There was little evidence of genuine desire for cooperation among equals. In this regard, Russian re-gionalism was reminiscent of US efforts to use the OAS during the Cold War and Nigeria's attempt to shelter its decision to intervene in Liberia under a multilateral umbrella.

A third cluster of self-interested interventions occurred in Central Africa in the 1990s. This phase began with the Rwandese Popular Front (RPF) invasion of northern Rwanda in 1990. Increas-ing Ugandan support of the RPF in the early 1990s in their insurgent challenge to the Habyarimana regime provoked counter-intervention by France, many of whose policy-makers viewed the RPF action as part of a more general struggle between the Anglo-Saxon and Francophone worlds in Central Africa. French troops were deployed in *Opération Noirot* in 1990. They provided logistics and communications support to Habyarimana's forces, and as-sisted with security behind the front. In addition, the French maintained and sometimes flew the government's helicopters and assisted in artillery positioning.[53] Despite a ceasefire agreement in 1993 (the Arusha Accords) that provided for power-sharing, dis-armament and the insertion of a UN peacekeeping force, the situation remained unstable, in part owing to the unhappiness of many in the incumbent Rwandan government with the concessions made to the RPF. In April 1994, the deaths of the presidents of Rwanda and Burundi in a plane crash unleashed a massive cam-paign of genocide against Tutsis and moderate Hutus.

The RPF resumed its offensive in the north and its eventual victory generated a flood of refugees and ex-government soldiers and militias into Zaire. There they reorganised and began incur-sions back into Rwanda. The response of the Rwandese govern-ment was to revive and support an eastern-Zairean Tutsi-based opposition group, the *Banyamulenge* (led by Laurent Kabila), which cleared the refugee camps at the end of 1996. The insurgents then rapidly moved west towards Kinshasa, attracting military support from other like-minded regional states along the way. Uganda provided substantial military support because it saw Mobutu as a longstanding opponent and because Rwanda was a regional ally. Angola entered because it sought an end to Zaire's harbouring of the Angolan opposition movement, UNITA. Namibia became involved because of its long historical ties to Angola and a desire for stability in that country. Zimbabwe also joined in, presumably in the hope of economic gain in the event of an insurgent victory. Zimbabwe's action also reflected its rivalry with Uganda and Rwanda for a leading role in Central Africa. In short, each country's rationale for intervention was self-interested. Zaire's neighbours sensed that it was doomed and wished to secure their political and economic share.

A year later, the victorious coalition fractured when Kabila acted to reduce Rwandese and Tutsi influence in his government and military. Rwanda and Uganda sought to depose the new government; Angola, Namibia, and Zimbabwe sought to sustain it. The situation deteriorated into a scramble for territory and resources, with the country being divided into an array of fiefdoms controlled by foreign armies and pro-government and opposition political groups. This evolution reflects the traditional pattern of intervention well. States intervened to control risk and to realise material gains in territory or resources, or political control. Their actions provoked counter-intervention and regional escalation.

Finally, there was the 1990s history of intervention in south and south-west Asia, a continuation of a pattern well established during the Cold War. After Soviet withdrawal in 1989, the Afghan *mujahiddin* coalition fractured, producing civil war. Pakistan (through its intelligence services, the ISI) backed a Taliban bid for power, both to mollify domestic Islamist opinion and to ensure that Afghanistan would not fall into hostile hands. Other neighbouring states lined up with anti-Taliban forces. Russia and Uzbekistan supported the coalition of groups that eventually became the Northern Alliance out of a desire to maintain control of northern Afghanistan, to distance threats of Islamic militancy from CIS borders and also to maintain the stabilisation of Tajikistan. India also supported the northern forces, seeking a friendly state on Pakistan's western borders as a means of applying further pressure on the latter. Iran, meanwhile, became involved in support of the Hazara minority in central Afghanistan, on grounds of religious affinity but also because the Iranians were radically opposed to the Sunni variant of political Islam predominant in Afghanistan. The result was a prolongation of the civil war and profound humanitarian crisis that endured until 2001.

Another element of the Afghan case that deserves mention was the interventionist role of transnational movements. In the mid-1990s, al-Qaeda took refuge in Afghanistan. In return for sanctuary, they provided substantial financial and military support to the Taliban in its war effort. This support altered the domestic political and military balance in favour of the Taliban. While doing so, they used Afghanistan as a base from which to plan and to mount a global campaign of terror. This culminated in the attack on the United States on 11 September 2001 and led to the US and coalition counter-intervention, which aimed both to eliminate al-Qaeda and to destroy the domestic political context that permitted its activities. This involved a decisive entry on the side of the Northern Alliance.

The other principal area of intervention in the region has been Kashmir, where the Pakistani government for many years gave sanctuary to, permitted the activities of, and reportedly actively supported the efforts of Islamic militants to destabilise Jammu and Kashmir, if not to detach it entirely from the Indian state. The reasons for this policy appeared to be both external and domestic. The Kashmir conflict was a central element of the regional rivalry between India and Pakistan dating back to the independence of the two countries in 1947. In addition, support for Islamist groups abroad appeased the radical opposition at home.

Looking at these regional cases as a group, several general characteristics were evident. First, and most obviously, in all of these cases the primary motivation of intervening states was power–political. They sought to alter domestic structures in target states in order to achieve relative gains *vis-à-vis* regional adversaries or to prevent the latter from achieving similar gains. Second, the normative elements that dominated Western discussion of intervention in the 1990s were conspicuously absent. In general, these intervening actors made little attempt to justify their actions in terms of universal norms of any kind. Their actions themselves often amounted to a negation of these norms. Third, except where such activities created substantial negative externalities for Western states (as in the former Yugoslavia), they were tolerated by the bearers of liberal norms. Indeed, in some circumstances (e.g., the support of Russian intervention in the CIS, or the effort to get rid of Joseph Mobutu), such activities were supported by major Western states.

Discussion of the interventionist activities of regional powers raises again the question of a bifurcation of the international system regarding the use of force. Earlier, it was suggested that the norm of humanitarian intervention was generally applied outside the Western core of the system. The discussion of multilateral practice confirmed this proposition, suggesting that multilateral intervention was a means whereby the Western great powers in particular coped with challenges elsewhere in the system. This discussion of the practice of regional powers indicates that in many (though not all) areas outside the transatlantic zone the practice of unilateral intervention remained common, its self-interested logic evident, and its normative content weak.

The mention of transnational groups leads to a final dimension of the evolution of intervention in the 1990s. The apparently increasing role of non-state actors drew into question the state-centricity of traditional analysis. The dominance of the state in matters of intervention was put into question not only from above (by the growing role of multilateral organisations), but from below (by private, transnational security companies providing support to governments facing serious internal challenges).[54] The principal examples of the latter in the 1990s were the role of Executive Outcomes (EO) in Angola, Sierra Leone and Papua-New Guinea (Bougainville) and that of Military Professional Resources Incorporated (MPRI) in Croatia and Bosnia in support of government armed forces.

However, several aspects of these engagements draw into question their importance for a general discussion of the evolution of intervention. First, the purchase of private military services is not new, but was a common pattern in the pre-Westphalian and early Westphalian international system. It reappeared in the role of mercenaries in the conflicts of post-independence Africa. Second, the practice is quite limited. All of the prominent cases were clustered in the early and mid-1990s and were confined to a very small number of states. Third, these services were contracted by governments, and so the involvement of these organisations is not a matter of intervention without consent of sovereign authorities.

Moreover, it is legitimate to question to what extent these organisations and their activities were non-state in character. In several instances, such as that of EO in Angola and Sierra Leone, the capacity for these companies to enter depended on the willingness of major state and interstate organisations to tolerate, if not to support their role. When, for example, the US government decided that the continuing presence of EO in Angola was an impediment to the peace process, President Clinton asked his Angolan counterpart to remove them. The firm left soon afterwards.[55] In addition, in the case of Sierra Leone, the capacity of a weak government presiding over a devastated economy to finance EO contracts depended on the use of money loaned by international organisations, where the principal decision-making power was held by the major member-states. The case of MPRI is simpler still. It was an enterprise made up in considerable measure of veterans of the US armed services and intelligence agencies who had close ties to the Department of Defense and to the CIA. Its business largely took the form of contracts from the US government for the provision of military assistance. That is to say, it was in important respects an agent of that government. Its actions reflected American policy towards the conflicts in question. Furthermore, over the past decade, strong consideration has been given to the possibility of multilateral organisations using private military companies in lieu of direct intervention. As the UK's Foreign Secretary put it recently: 'A strong and reputable private military sector might have a role in enabling the UN to respond more rapidly and effectively in crises'.[56]

Finally, the operations of these corporations to a degree depended on the good will of the countries in which they were based. When the government of South Africa, for example, began to worry about the activities of EO, it introduced a law that required prior government authorisation of each operation. This greatly complicated EO's affairs. In general, therefore, one could say that the interventionist activities of private enterprises do not constitute a significant challenge to the centrality of the state.

Conclusion

Looking at the broader history of intervention in world politics, there is considerable variation in its normative dimension. In the Westphalian system, five normative currents were evident. One was non-interventionism, the view that state sovereignty and recognition implied that states accepted (or should accept) an obligation not to interfere in the domestic affairs of other states and that there were no exceptions to this principle. The example of the UN General Assembly declaration on intervention provided a good example, as did the declaration of the non-aligned movement in reaction to the notion of humanitarian intervention. In its absolute form, however, this perspective was historically rare.

This approach encountered several types of objection. One (usually conservative) was that intervention was permissible when events within a state threatened the fabric of order between states. A second (liberal) was that intervention was permitted when a state systematically violated the rights of its citizens or is incapable of protecting them. This view slid into the position that the applicability of the principle of non-intervention depended on 'standards of civilisation' – that is to say that 'civilised' states enjoyed the protection of the norm whereas non-civilised states or polities did not (see below). Finally, there was the pragmatic view that there could, or should, be no general rule of intervention, but that states might be entitled to intervene in specific circumstances when their core interests were threatened.

There have been periods of extremely active conflict between these perspectives; there have been others in which a degree of consensus favouring one or another principle prevailed. The influence of these various normative perspectives in international society varied in response to the historical context and, in particular, to systemic or regional distributions of power and the emergence of revolutionary challenges to the international status quo.

There has also been wide variation in the relationship between norms and practice. There were periods in which there appeared to be a reasonably close fit between the two, but there have also been times when the practice of intervention appeared to bear little relation to the evolving normative framework. Although there may have been durable developments in related normative areas (e.g., the embedding of human rights in international law), the evolving history of intervention has been variable and cyclical in nature rather than heading forward in a clearly defined direction.

However, there were important changes in the form and content of intervention after the Cold War. Earlier interventions were generally statist and unilateral. During the Cold War, they were motivated principally by the self-interested pursuit of political advantage in a bipolar pluralist framework. The normative and legal contexts were ambiguous. On the one hand, solidarist norms were gradually becoming embedded in international law. On the other hand, the proscription of intervention had become stronger. Indeed, the principle of non-intervention was arguably far more forceful in this period than in earlier ones, when the proscription of the practice was commonly mitigated by considerations of self-defence or of what might constitute a legitimate internal structure of governance. In any event, the normative framework had little to do with the practice of intervention during the Cold War.

After the Cold War, and in the context of the transformation of war, the disappearance of the bipolar competition for power and the establishment of American hegemony, intervention became increasingly multilateral in form. The notion that sovereignty was conditional, and based on state performance in protecting the rights of citizens, became increasingly influential. The legal proscription of intervention became weaker in consequence.

Intervention had a stronger normative component in the 1990s than it did in the Cold War era. Moreover, the normative content of post-Cold War intervention was different. Collective values of conflict resolution, the protection of human rights and to some extent the promotion of democracy gained influence at the expense of more clearly self-interested political objectives. Much intervention in the post-Cold War era was embedded in the interpretation of international humanitarian and human rights law and was frequently authorised by international organisations (notably the United Nations) empowered to mandate the use of force.

However, before concluding that statist pluralism was disappearing in the face of human solidarity and rampant multilateralism, several reservations are necessary. First, normatively based challenges to the sovereign rights of states are hardly new in international history, as the quick review above of the struggle between Protestants and Catholics in Europe in the fifteenth and sixteenth centuries, the interventionist proclivities of the French revolutionaries, the conservative position of the Holy Alliance in the first half of the nineteenth century and the flirtation with humanitarian intervention throughout that century reveals. Perhaps more significantly, in the nineteenth century the legitimacy of intervention in polities outside the European Concert was not questioned. Since these states were not part of the Concert, they were not protected by Concert norms. To the extent that the intrusion of the imperial powers into the affairs on non-European polities was justified at all, such justification tended to be expressed in terms of civilisation, focusing on the *mission civilisatrice* of Europe to bring its values to the less fortunate peoples of what came to be known as the Third World. This ideological justification for self-interested power projection bears a resemblance to the contemporary notion that societies that do not honour Western liberal practices regarding governance and rights are legitimate targets of reformative international action.

In these respects, the absolutisation of sovereignty and the interpretation of the principle of non-intervention that developed during the Cold War were historically atypical. And even in the Cold War era, this absolutisation was mitigated to some extent by evidence of emergence of a norm concerning the permissibility of 'dictatorial interference' regarding struggles for national self-determination.

Second, where humanitarian issues did come into play in the 1990s, the effort to obtain consent from sovereign authorities remained significant. International society was reluctant to intervene in domestic jurisdiction without it, despite the human rights justifications for intrusion. The reluctance to embrace a universal norm of this type was evident also in the care that the UN Security Council took to underline the exceptional quality of cases in which the use of force for humanitarian purposes was mandated. This caution reflected the fact that the normative evolution was strongly contested by a coalition that included two permanent members of the Security Council (Russia and China), as well as most states in the South.

Third, and turning to practice, the selectivity of intervention in humanitarian crises suggested that pluralist political interest continued to play a significant role in decision-making. The nature of interest, however, was quite different from the Cold War era. Whereas during the Cold War and in earlier periods intervention by the great powers tended to be motivated by systemically determined interest (e.g., the balance of power and relative gain *vis-à-vis* rival great powers), the interests informing great power intervention in the 1990s tended to be more diffuse (e.g., the prevention of, or control of, flows of migration and the effort to limit the spread of conflict and to address problems of criminality). Moreover, given the absence of a grand strategic imperative, public opinion and domestic politics played a more prominent role in decisions to intervene. Intervention was in this sense a means of responding to domestic political challenges as much as it was one of managing the international system.

Fourth, instances of unilateral and self-interested intervention persisted in many regions of the world outside the West. Here, the practice of intervention displayed a much more traditional character as one means among many that states used to manage threats in their environment or to take advantage of opportunities created by developments in neighbouring states. Normative justification in such cases was weak if not absent, as was normative constraint.

This suggests that – with regard to intervention – the international system has sustained its Cold War bifurcation, where in a 'zone of peace' the practice is highly constrained, while elsewhere it remains a reasonably common state practice.

Perhaps the most significant transformation in the politics of intervention was the marked reduction in the frequency of unilateral intervention by the great powers and their growing reluctance to intervene without justification in terms of widely shared normative principles. Political interest continued to play a significant role in contemporary intervention by the major powers. But these powers now appeared to be compelled to justify their actions in terms of general principles and they rarely intervened in the internal affairs of other states without authorisation based on these general principles from authoritative multilateral institutions. Although the causal weight of these principles in determining their behaviour was contestable, this did limit their flexibility in contemplating intervention for egoistic reasons.

Afterword

Somewhat ironically, the post-Cold War decade, in which solidarist norms were such a focus of attention in discussion of intervention, was bracketed by two similar events that reflected quite traditional patterns of political intervention. In 1989, the United States reacted to the emergence of a military leader in Panama who was deeply involved in transnational narcotics trafficking to the United States and whose followers were attacking American personnel and threatening American facilities by dispatching an expeditionary force that ousted him and restored constitutional authority. They arrested Manuel Noriega and remanded him to trial in Miami. He was found guilty of drug-related offences and was imprisoned. In 2001, the United States reacted to an attack by a transnational terrorist movement on the World Trade Center by attacking Afghanistan, overthrowing the government that harboured al-Qaeda, arrested large numbers of Taliban and al-Qaeda personnel, and transported them to Guatanamo Bay, where their fate was to be considered by military tribunals established for the purpose.

Both of these interventions were self-interested. Both

removed a hostile government and replaced it with one more amenable to US interests. Neither displayed any particular commitment to solidarist norms. The latter were largely irrelevant to the Panamian case. In Afghanistan, although American policy-makers recognised the gravity of the humanitarian situation in Afghanistan, it was not a major motivating factor for their action. By many accounts, US military action displayed less commitment to norms of discrimination in war than might have been expected.[1] American military action complicated the humanitarian response by international agencies and NGOs. US officers were careful to ensure that humanitarian concerns did not upset the pursuit of political and military objectives. The humanitarian efforts of US and allied forces were minimal during the conflict. The United States steered clear of participation in the UN-mandated peace-keeping force in Afghanistan, preferring instead to focus on the elimination of remaining Taliban and al-Qaeda units and (most recently) on assistance to the transitional government in the face of growing opposition from disaffected warlords and their forces.[2]

The two events differed from earlier patterns of intervention in one key respect. American intervention in Panama was provoked in some measure by a transnational process – narco-trafficking. The Afghan case was principally motivated by the desire to address a transnational non-state threat. In both instances, removing a government was perceived to be a necessary aspect of dealing with a transnational process. One might expect that intervention in years to come may reflect not so much an effort to seek or maintain influence within a state by interfering with its political process, but a concern to manage the more negative aspects of globalisation.

There was also one key difference between the two cases. The United States made little effort to situate its activities in Panama within a multilateral institutional framework, and ignored the United Nations completely. In Afghanistan, however, the United States sought and obtained a UN Security Council mandate for its actions, although it was arguably not obliged to do so.[3] Moreover, it received a full endorsement of its military response from NATO, which invoked Article V of the North Atlantic Treaty for the first time in its history. In these respects, the Afghan case appeared to reinforce the principal argument of the previous chapter – that intervening states are increasingly constrained to legitimise their actions in and through multilateral organisations.

However, American activities surrounding the Afghanistan war displayed an increasing propensity to unilateralism, both in decisions on the campaign and on the treatment of detainees. The United States, meanwhile, broadened the campaign by intervening in the civil conflict in the southern Philippines and by sending special forces troops, helicopters and trainers to Georgia to assist that country in its campaign to reassert control over the Pankisi Gorge, a region of the country in which Chechen fighters, allegedly with links to al-Qaeda, were active. In the 2002 State of the Union speech, President Bush identified an 'axis of evil' made up of Iraq, Iran and North Korea. This was accompanied by clear signals that the United States was contemplating intervention in Iraq to remove Saddam Hussein. Options in the latter case were reported to include 'invasion, support for a local insurgency, backing for a coup and possible combinations of these alternatives'.[4]

This prospect and the broader 'struggle against evil' evoked acrimonious comment from America's French and German allies, as well as from the European Commission. Such responses suggested that the United States would have difficulty in generating new mandates for such action. To the extent that these obstacles prevent multilateral authorisation, the international system's most powerful actor may deem it necessary to depart from the multilateral framework.

It would be rash to identify a trend on the basis of one case. But, as we have seen, both the frequency and the normative content of intervention have been highly variable over time. The emergence of revolutionary forces in the international system (as, for example, during the period of the French revolution) tends to increase the incidence of the practice and to accentuate its political content. This suggests that the growing normative constraints on the unilateral exercise of power and the increasing role of solidarist concerns over justice apparently evident in the post-Cold War history of intervention may gradually attenuate in a movement back towards a more statist, unilateralist and power-political international system.

Notes

Introduction

1 Solidarism implies that states accept a responsibility not only to protect the security of their own people, but to defend human rights everywhere. See Jennifer Welsh, 'From Right to Responsibility: Humanitarian Intervention and International Society', Global Governance (forthcoming, 2002).

2 Rosalyn Higgins, 'Intervention and International Law', in Hedley Bull (ed.), *Intervention in World Politics* (Oxford: Oxford University Press, 1984), p. 34. Ian Brownlie dates this development to 'at least 1965' in *Principles of Public International Law*, 3rd edition (Oxford: Clarendon Press, 1979), pp. 596–598.

3 Nicholas Wheeler, *Saving Strangers: Humanitarian Intervention in International Society* (Oxford: Oxford University Press, 2000), p. 8. I take humanitarian norms (which focus on the rights of survival and to dignity) to be a subset of human rights.

4 Kofi Annan, 'Two Concepts of Sovereignty', *The Economist*, 18 September 1999, p. 82.

5 Hedley Bull, 'Introduction', in Bull, *Intervention in World Politics*, p. 2.

6 Adam Roberts, *Humanitarian Action in War*, Adelphi Paper 305 (Oxford: Oxford University Press for the IISS, 1996), p. 19.

7 See the comprehensive bibliography in International Commission on Intervention and State Sovereignty, *The Responsibility to Protect*, Volume II (Research, Bibliography, Background) (Ottawa: IDRC, 2002), pp. 227–336, where this emphasis is amply evident.

8 American intervention in Haiti in 1994, for example, was justified in terms of the restoration of democracy, but was substantially motivated by a desire to stem the tide of migration from Haiti to Florida. The stated justification required the reinstatement of the elected president, Bertrand Aristide, despite the strong reservations in some American official circles concerning his suitability.

Chapter 1

1 For a more complete discussion of the definition of intervention, see Hedley Bull, 'Introduction', p. 1.

2 See Higgins, 'Intervention and International Law', p. 32.

3 John Chipman, *French Military*

Policy and African Security, Adelphi Paper 201 (London: IISS, 1985), p. 9.

[4] *Ibid.*, pp. 7–9.

[5] Stanley Hoffmann, 'The Problem of Intervention', in Bull, *Intervention in World Politics,* pp. 7–8. See also S. Neil MacFarlane, *Intervention and Regional Security,* Adelphi Paper 196 (London: IISS, 1985), pp. 1–2.

[6] James Rosenau, 'Intervention as a Scientific Concept', *Journal of Conflict Resolution* vol. XIII, no. 2, 1969, p. 153.

[7] Roberts, *Humanitarian Action in War,* p. 8.

[8] Hall, cited in R.J. Vincent, *Nonintervention and International Order* (Princeton, NJ: Princeton University Press, 1974), p. 13.

[9] Tom J. Farer and Felice Gaer, 'The UN and Human Rights', in Adam Roberts and Benedict Kingsbury (eds.), *United Nations, Divided World: The UN's Roles in International Relations* (Oxford: Oxford University Press, 1993), p. 242.

[10] It should be noted, however, that such normative concerns applied not to humanity as a whole, but to Christian (and European) subjects of a non-Christian polity. To judge from Germany's systematic massacre of the Herrero and Nama in south-west Africa, they did not apply to non-European Christians whose rights were being violated by a European great power. See Thomas Pakenham, *The Scramble for Africa* (New York: Random House, 1991), pp. 602–615. Even less did they apply to non-Christians. The latter point is evident in the inaction of the Great Powers in the face of the massive cruelties perpetrated by the authorities occupying and exploiting the Congo on behalf of King Leopold of Belgium.

[11] Francis Deng, *Sovereignty as Responsibility* (Washington, DC: Brookings, 1995).

[12] Vincent's characterisation is symptomatic. He suggests that intervention is traditionally understood to be the participation of a state in a conflict taking place within another state. Vincent, *Nonintervention*, p. 6.

[13] It is noteworthy, however, that such companies played a prominent role in the international relations of Europe in the late medieval and early modern period.

[14] In January–February, 2002, the latter point was highlighted in the confusion over whether the laws of war applied to Taliban and al-Qaeda prisoners taken by the Americans to Guantanamo Bay in Cuba.

Chapter 2

[1] See Thucydides, *History of the Peloponnesian War* (Harmondsworth, Penguin, 1986), pp. 49–53.

[2] For a more complete characterisation of the Hellenic states system, see Martin Wight, *Systems of States* (Leicester: Leicester University Press, 1977), pp. 46–72.

[3] Thucydides, *The Peloponnesian War*, p. 402.

[4] As Paul Kennedy put it: 'By 1659, when Spain finally acknowledged defeat in the Treaty of the Pyrenees, the political *plurality* of Europe was an established fact'. Paul Kennedy, *The Rise and Fall of the Great Powers* (New York: Random House, 1987), p. 31.

[5] Indeed, the pre-Westphalian period is an early instance of a recurrent pattern in which revolutionary transformation of the international system (in this instance the transition to a

pluralist structure) brings a dramatic increase in the incidence of intervention.

[6] This is not to say that major interventions were unknown. One of the more significant was Tsar Alexis' intervention on behalf of the Ukrainian Cossacks in their revolt against Poland in 1654, which eventually resulted in Russian acquisition of Ukraine.

[7] Hugo Grotius, for example, argued that intervention in the face of atrocities committed by a ruler against his own people might be justifiable. See Wheeler, *Saving Strangers*, p. 45. Arguably, moreover, Kant's *Perpetual Peace* implies a right to intervention when the political rights of a people were being denied by a despotic regime. Vincent, *Nonintervention*, pp. 57–58.

[8] *Ibid.*, p. 12, 67.

[9] Cited in Edward Gulick, *Europe's Classical Balance of Power* (New York: Norton, 1967), p. 63.

[10] Hajo Holborn, 'Russia and the European Political System', in Ivo Lederer (ed.), *Russian Foreign Policy: Essays in Historical Perspective* (New Haven: Yale University Press, 1962), p. 383.

[11] Derek McKay and H.M. Scott, *The Rise of the Great Powers* (London: Longman, 1983), p. 326.

[12] Henry Kissinger, *A World Restored: Metternich, Castlereagh and the Problems of Peace 1812–1822* (Boston: Houghton Mifflin, 1954), Sentry Edition, pp. 265, 275.

[13] See Torbjörn Knutsen, *A History of International Relations Theory* (Manchester: Manchester University Press, 1992), pp. 152–153. This dissension extended to the United States as well, where leading international lawyers criticised Holy Alliance interventions as violations of the 'perfect equality and entire independence of all distinct states', but accepted that in practice the right of interposition depended 'on the circumstances of the case'. Vincent, *Nonintervention*, pp. 33–34.

[14] Gerrit Gong, *The Standard of 'Civilization' in International Society* (Oxford: Clarendon, 1984), pp. 55–56.

[15] *Ibid.*, p. 52.

[16] Kissinger, *A World Restored*, pp. 288–289.

[17] *Ibid.*, p. 295.

[18] Wheeler, *Saving Strangers*, p. 46.

[19] On this point, see Vincent, *Nonintervention*, p. 87.

[20] Some authors do fully discount its significance. A noted international legal scholar, for example, once suggested that reference to humanitarian intervention in Greece in 1827 was an example of 'post-factoism'. See Ian Brownlie, 'Humanitarian Intervention', in John Norton Moore (ed.), *Law and Civil War in the Modern World* (Baltimore, MD: Johns Hopkins University Press, 1974), p. 220.

[21] Kissinger, *A World Restored*, p. 279; Vincent, *Nonintervention*, p. 93.

[22] The Monroe Doctrine asserted an American right to ensure that no European power gained undue influence in the western hemisphere. The Roosevelt Corollary suggested that in instances where the actions of local states risked provoking extra-regional engagement, the United States could legitimately intervene to maintain order in the hemisphere and to ensure that the interests of outside powers were satisfied.

[23] See Ruhl J. Bartlett (ed.), *The Record of American Diplomacy: Documents and Readings in the History of American Foreign Relations*, 4th Edition (New York, Alfred A. Knopf, 1964), p. 539; and Walter LaFeber, *The American*

Age: U.S. Foreign Policy at Home and Abroad: Volume I – to 1920 (New York: Norton, 1994), pp. 197–202, 206–212, 239–250.

24 Walter LaFeber, *Inevitable Revolutions* (New York: Norton, 1983), p. 50.

25 LaFeber, *The American Age*, p. 279.

26 Vincent, *Nonintervention*, p. 147.

27 British intervention in Russia is masterfully treated by Richard Ullman in *Anglo–Soviet Relations* (London: Oxford University Press and Princeton: Princeton University Press, 1961–1972), Volume 1, *Intervention and the War* and Volume 2, *Britain and the Russian Civil War*.

Chapter 3

1 For a discussion of intervention during this period, see MacFarlane, *Intervention and Regional Security*. See also Zaki Laïdi, *Les contraintes d'une rivalité: Les superpuissances et l'Afrique (1960–1985)* (Paris: La Découverte, 1986).

2 GA Res. 217 (III)A, 10 December 1948.

3 See Tom Farer and Felice Gaer, 'The UN and Human Rights: At the End of the Beginning', in Adam Roberts and Benedict Kingsbury, *United Nations, Divided World: The UN's Roles in International Relations* (Oxford: Oxford University Press, 1993), pp. 240–296; and David Forsythe, *Human Rights in World Politics* (Lincoln, Nebraska: University of Nebraska Press, 1989).

4 For the text, see Adam Roberts and Richard Guelff, *Documents on the Laws of War*, 2nd edition (Oxford: Oxford University Press, 1989), pp. 449–458. The Protocol came into force on 7 December 1978.

5 Signed 9 December 1948, came into force 12 January 1951. The Convention establishes that genocide is a crime under international law and that signatory states accept the responsibility of preventing or punishing it (Article 1).

6 Signed 4 November 1950, came into force September 1953. The principal aim of the Convention was to create a mechanism to implement the Universal Declaration of 1948. Text available at www.echr.coe.int/Eng/BasicTexts.htm

7 Signed 22 November 1969, came into force 18 July 1978. For the text see www.oas.org

8 There was also considerable debate regarding the possibility of intervention to promote the right of peoples to self-determination. See, for example, 'Declaration on Friendly Relations'. This development was, however, hotly contested by the colonial powers and the United States.

9 There are two important exceptions: sanctions against Southern Rhodesia concerning the unilateral declaration of independence by that colony of the UK (1966–79) and the arms embargo against South Africa over the issue of apartheid (1977–1994). Both cases raise the possibility that coercive action – if not intervention – intended to affect the domestic conduct of states might be permissible where that conduct violated the principle of national self-determination. See, *inter alia*, Margaret P. Doxey, *United Nations Sanctions: Current Policy Issues* (Halifax: Centre for Foreign Policy Studies of Dalhousie University, 1997), pp. 1–3.

10 Indeed, the UN had huge difficulty with the prior question of coming up with an agreed definition of aggression. The General Assembly adopted a 'Resolution on the Definition of

Aggression' (A/9631, 1975) in December 1974.

[11] UNGA, 'Declaration on the Inadmissibility of Intervention in the Domestic Affairs of States and the Protection of Their Independence and Sovereignty' (Resolution no. 2131, 21 December 1965); and UNGA, 'Declaration on Principles of International Law concerning Friendly Relations and Cooperation among States' (Resolution no. 2625, 24 October 1970).

[12] Declarations and resolutions of the General Assembly are not 'hard law', but when the majority supporting an act of the Assembly is particularly large or is unanimous one might conclude that the act in question reflects international custom, which is recognised as a source of law.

[13] International Court of Justice, 'Corfu Channel Case (Merits): Judgement of 9 April 1949', posted at www.icj-cij.org/icjwww/idecisions/isummaries/iccsummary490409.htm

[14] Rosalyn Higgins, 'Internal War and International Law', in Richard Falk and Cyril Black (eds), *The Future of the International Legal Order*, Volume 3 (Princeton, NJ: Princeton University Press, 1971), p. 106. However, Higgins presaged a post-Cold War development by suggesting that a humanitarian intervention would be legal in the event that it was authorised by the Security Council in response to an identified threat to international peace and security.

[15] Sergei Kovalev, 'International Obligations of Socialist Countries', *Pravda*, 26 September 1968, p. 4.

[16] Raymond Aron, *Peace and War: A Theory of International Relations* (Malabar, FL: Robert E. Krieger, 1981), p. 118.

[17] Derek Bowett, 'The Interrelation of Theories of Intervention and Self-Defense', in Moore (ed.), *Law and Civil War*, p. 42.

[18] Akehurst, 'Humanitarian Intervention', p. 95.

[19] Concerning the declarations of the General Assembly, Rosalyn Higgins noted that: 'Certainly many states regard it in practice as entirely acceptable to bring various pressures to bear to influence the internal or external events of other states. One thus has constantly the problem of identifying the reality, and measuring it against the rhetoric'. Higgins, 'Intervention and International Law', p. 38. Raymond Aron recognised the same difficulty more sharply: 'Since international law ... is based on the sovereignty and the equality of states, it is not a reflection but a negation of the present reality'. Aron, *Peace and War*, p. 567.

[20] French and Belgian troops were delivered to Kolwezi by aircraft of the US Military Airlift Command. Chipman *French Military Policy and African Security*, pp. 13, 43–44.

[21] For useful discussions of French military policy and intervention in Africa, see Dominique Moïsi et Pierre Lellouche, 'French Policy in Africa: A Lonely Battle against Destabilization', *International Security*, Spring 1979; John Chipman, *French Military Power and African Security*; and John Chipman, *French Power in Africa* (Oxford: Basil Blackwell, 1989).

[22] Thomas O'Toole, *The Central African Republic* (Boulder, CO: Westview Press, 1986), p. 55. This action had a humanitarian component, since it followed the slaughter of 150–200 schoolchildren by government forces in a dispute over mandatory school uniforms. That said, it seems likely that the

principal motivation was the fact that the increasingly erratic emperor had become a substantial embarrassment to the French.

[23] Jane Boulden, *Peace Enforcement: The United Nations Experience in Congo, Somalia, and Bosnia* (Westport, CT: Praeger, 2000), pp. 23–24.

[24] Albert Hourani, *A History of the Arab Peoples* (New York: Warner, 1992), p. 411.

[25] One should also note that India's invasion was preceded by Pakistani air attacks on Indian territory.

[26] For discussion, see Wheeler, *Saving Strangers*, pp. 55–128.

[27] See Leo Kuper, *Genocide: Its Political Use in the Twentieth Century* (New Haven: Yale University Press, 1981), pp. 173–174.

[28] Amnesty International, *Political Killings by Governments* (London: Amnesty International, 1983), p. 44.

[29] UN Document, S/PV.2109 (1979), p. 4.

[30] See Jane Boulden, *Peace Enforcement: The United Nations Experience in Congo, Somalia, and Bosnia* (Westport, CT: Praeger, 2001), pp. 21–50. The other example from the period is that of UNFICYP in Cyprus (1964 to the present). However, the UN response was of the classic Chapter VI variety, and since coercion was not involved it does not fall within the category of intervention as that is defined here.

[31] *Ibid.*, pp. 29, 31.

[32] See Georges Abi-Saab, *The United Nations Operation in the Congo* (Oxford: Oxford University Press, 1978); and Conor Cruise O'Brien, *To Katanga and Back* (New York: Grosset and Dunlap, 1962).

[33] For example, given the difficulties of the process of decolonisation

and the growing pressure to accelerate the process, Britain was reluctant to create precedents for UN intervention in matters of domestic jurisdiction.

[34] See Eric Berman and Katie Sams, *Peacekeeping in Africa: Capabilities and Culpabilities* (New York: United Nations, 2000), pp. 47–56.

Chapter 4

[1] *Pravda*, 7 December 1988.

Chapter 5

[1] For useful discussion of the character of contemporary war, see Pierre Hassner, *Violence and Peace: From the Atomic Bomb to Ethnic Cleansing* (London: Central European University Press, 1997); and Mary Kaldor, *New and Old Wars: Organised Violence in a Global Era* (Cambridge: Polity, 1999).

[2] Roberts, *Humanitarian Action in War*, p. 12. Between 1995 and 2000, the number of refugees dropped, but remained well above the level characteristic of the 1970s and 1980s. As of 31 December 1999, UNHCR indicated that there were 22.3 million people of concern globally, of which over 11 million were refugees. See www/unhcr.ch

[3] Roberta Cohen and Francis Deng, *The Forsaken People: Case Studies of the Internally Displaced* (Washington: Brookings, 1998), p. 1. UNHCR believed that the figure in 2001 was between 20 and 25 million. See www.unhcr.ch

[4] Adam Roberts, 'More Refugees, Less Asylum: A Regime in Transformation', *Journal of Refugee Studies* vol. 11, no. 4, 1998, pp. 375–395.

[5] S/23500 (Statement by the President of the Council) (31 January 1992).

[6] Boutros Boutros-Ghali, *An Agenda for Peace: Preventive Diplomacy,*

'Peacemaking and Peacekeeping'
(New York: United Nations, 1992),
paragraphs 1–19.

[7] Kofi Annan, 'Reflections on
Intervention', 35th Ditchley
Foundation Lecture (26 June
1998), in *The Question of
Intervention: Statements by the
Secretary-General* (New York:
United Nations, 1999), p. 6.

[8] As Boutros-Ghali's predecessor,
Javier Perez de Cuellar, declared
in 1991: 'It is now increasingly
felt that the principle of
non-interference with the
domestic jurisdiction of States
cannot be regarded as a protective
barrier behind which human
rights could be massively or
systematically violated'. See
'Report of the Secretary General
on the Work of the Organization',
A/46/1, 1991.

[9] See Mario Betatti and Bernard
Kouchner, *Le devoir d'ingérence*
(Paris: Denoël, 1987); and Mario
Bettati, *Le droit d'ingérence:
Mutation de l'ordre international*
(Paris: Odile Jacob, 1996).

[10] S/Res/688 (5 April 1991). France,
the UK, and the USA
simultaneously pursued a
trilateral initiative outside the
context of the Security Council. In
the first three weeks of April
1991, their airforces made 875
flights into Iraqi airspace to
deliver relief to displaced Kurds
in the mountains of north-western
Iraq. They also delivered supplies
by helicopter and truck across the
frontier, using military personnel
and logistics. This intrusion took
place without the consent of the
Iraqi authorities and the Iraqi
government strongly protested at
what it perceived to be an
intervention in its internal affairs
that was prohibited in
international law.

[11] S/Res/733 (23 January 1992).

[12] S/Res/746 (17 March 1992);

S/Res/751 (24 April 1992);
S/Res/775 (28 August 1992).

[13] S/Res/794 (3 December 1992). For
a comprehensive discussion of the
debates of the council on Somalia,
see Neil Fenton, *Consent, Coercion
and Sovereignty in United Nations
Security Council Mandated
Operations, 1991–5*, D.Phil. Thesis,
Oxford University, 2000,
pp. 146–178.

[14] S/Res/929 (22 June 1994).

[15] S/Res/940 (31 July 1994). For a
discussion of the debates and
actions of the council concerning
the crisis in Haiti, see David
Malone, *Decision-Making in the UN
Security Council: The Case of Haiti,
1990–1997* (Oxford: Clarendon
Press, 1998).

[16] S/Res/1132 (8 October 1997).

[17] In the case of East Timor,
however, Indonesian sovereignty
over the territory had never been
accepted by the United Nations.
For a general discussion, see
Richard Caplan, *A New
Trusteeship? The International
Administration of War-torn
Territories*, Adelphi Paper 341
(Oxford: Oxford University Press
for the IISS, 2002).

[18] See Mayall, *The New
Interventionism*, pp. 3–4. See also
DUPI, *Humanitarian Intervention:
Legal and Political Aspects*
(Copenhagen: DUPI, 1999), p. 17;
and The International
Commission in Intervention and
State Sovereignty, *The
Responsibility to Protect* (Ottawa:
IDRC, 2002), p. XI.

[19] Sir David Hannay, cited in
Fenton, *Consent, Coercion and
Sovereignty*, p. 170.

[20] The significance of this consent is
itself problematic, as it arguably
contravened the Haitian
constitution.

[21] Adam Roberts notes that: 'Russia
and China had consistently made
it clear that they would veto any

proposal for military action against Yugoslavia regarding its conduct in its own territory.' See 'NATO's 'Humanitarian War' over Kosovo', *Survival*, vol. 41, no. 3, Autumn 1999, p. 104.

22 *Ibid.*, pp. 106–7: 'In this perspective it cannot be right to tolerate acts which violate widely supported legal norms just because the Charter does not explicitly provide for military action in such circumstances, or because a veto on the Security Council makes UN-authorised action impossible.'

23 Independent International Commission on Kosovo, *The Kosovo Report: Conflict, International Response, Lessons Learned* (Oxford: Oxford University Press, 2000), p. 4.

24 See www.nam.gov.za/minmeet/ newyorkcom.htm, paragraph 171. This sentence is repeated exactly in the 'Declaration of the Summit of the South,' adopted at the Havana summit of the G-77 in April, 2000. See www.nam.gov.za/ documentation/southdecl.htm, paragraph 54.

25 Cited in Evgenii Petrov, 'Doktrina Putina', *Nezavisimaya Gazeta* (electronic version), 2 February 2000.

26 'Moscow Joint Statement of the Heads of State of Russia and China' (18 July 2001 – 1347–18–07–2001), section 7.

27 See Vladimir Baranovsky, 'Humanitarian Intervention: Russia's Approaches', Paper delivered at the 2nd Pugwash Conference on Intervention, Sovereignty and International Security (28–30 September 2000), pp. 6–9.

28 S. Neil MacFarlane, 'What the International Community Can Do to Settle the [Chechen] Conflict', *Central Asia and the Caucasus*, no.

4, 2000.

29 In Russia's case, dilution of the principle of Security Council authorisation would erode one of the few remaining attributes of its great power status. Baranovsky, 'Humanitarian Intervention', p. 9.

30 See Wheeler and Dunne, 'East Timor and the New Humanitarian Interventionism', p. 809: 'ASEAN has consistently defended a view of sovereignty whereby the rights of states are largely decoupled from a duty to comply with humanitarian standards'.

31 One must recognise, however, that in a number of cases, 'consent' was less than freely given. For example, Indonesia consented to the deployment of INTERFET, a coalition force led by Australia, under considerable pressure from international financial institutions and key states such as the US.

32 More recently, several resolutions of the Security Council have omitted references to the specificity and uniqueness of the cases where the UN was considering the issue of intervention. One such instance was resolution 1132 (1997) on the intervention of ECOWAS to re-establish the democratically elected government of Sierra Leone after a *coup d'état*.

33 This conclusion applied first and foremost to situations in which the suspension of sovereignty was under discussion. In 1996, James Mayall noted that there was very little support in the Third World or in Western countries for the creation of protectorates. Mayall, *The New Interventionism*, p. 23. The occasional discussion that the Trusteeship Council might be revived for this purpose has as yet gone nowhere.

34 The relevant UNSC resolutions for Georgia (937–1994) and for

Tajikistan (968–1994) do not specifically authorise CIS actions. In the first instance, S/Res/937 (1994) notes that the CIS deployment occurred with the consent of all parties and states the UN's appreciation for CIS cooperation in facilitating UNOMIG. In the second, S/Res/968 (1994) 'positively acknowledge[s]' CIS contributions to conflict resolution.

[35] Thomas G. Weiss and Cindy Collins, *Humanitarian Challenges and Intervention*, 2nd edition (Boulder, Westview, 2000), p. 103.

[36] James Mayall noted in this context that 'by the end of 1993 there were clear signs that the governments of the major powers were more interested in limiting than in extending their international commitments'. James Mayall, *The New Interventionism*, p. 1.

[37] Former Secretary-General Boutros Boutros-Ghali maintains that he was shown a copy 'later'. See 'Report of the Independent Inquiry into the Actions of the UN during the 1994 Genocide in Rwanda', S/1999/1257 (15 December 1999).

[38] See the discussion in Philip Gourevitch, *We Wish to Inform You That Tomorrow We Will Be Killed with Our Families* (New York: Picador, 1998), pp. 152–154, for a characterisation of US perspectives on this issue.

[39] S/Res/918 (17 May 1994).

[40] S/Res/929 (22 June 1994).

[41] Gérard Prunier, *The Rwanda Crisis: History of a Genocide* (London: Hurst and Company, 1995), p. 282. See also pp. 285–286, where Prunier suggests that the decision on location of the deployment was influenced by the desire to have a large surviving victim population accessible to accompanying television cameras:

'A humanitarian intervention in a place where there was no longer anybody left to save would indeed have been embarrassing'.

[42] This list is not exhaustive. There is evidence of small-scale engagement of Russian troops in the Nagorno–Karabakh conflict on the Armenian side. In addition, when Russian forces left the Karabakh capital, they left their heavy weapons behind in the hands of the Karabakh Armenians. See S. Neil MacFarlane and Larry Minear, *Humanitarian Action and Politics: The Case of Nagorno-Karabakh*, Occasional Paper no. 25 (Providence, RI: The Watson Institute, 1997), pp. 29–30.

[43] For a very useful analysis of the Moldovan conflict, and Russia's role therein, see Charles King, 'Moldova with a Russian Face', *Foreign Policy*, no. 97, Winter 1994–5.

[44] For a discussion of the origins of civil conflict in Georgia in the 1990s, see S. Neil MacFarlane with George Khutsishvili, 'Ethnic Conflict in Georgia', in Symeon Giannakos (ed.), *Ethnic Conflict: Religion, Identity, and Politics* (Athens, OH: Ohio University Press, 2002).

[45] In his July, 2001 report on the conflict, the Secretary-General commented that 'meaningful negotiations on the future political status of Abkhazia within the State of Georgia have not yet begun'. 'Report of the Secretary General concerning the Situation in Abkhazia, Georgia', S/2001/713 (19 July 2001).

[46] 'Report of the Secretary-General concerning the Situation in Abkhazia, Georgia', S/2001/1008 (24 October 2001).

[47] It would be incorrect, however, to attribute full blame on the Russian Federation. Their

influence over the Abkhaz *de facto* authorities was not complete, and the intransigence of the parties poses the most significant obstacle to settlement. At the time of writing, for example, the Abkhaz side is refusing to participate in discussions of the political status of the territory, considering the question moot, subsequent to Abkhazia's 'Act of Independence' in 1999.

48 Although the force contained Uzbek and Kazakh units, it was overwhelmingly Russian in composition.

49 As Russia's Foreign Policy Concept (1993) put it: 'Without [resolution of the problem of the external borders of the CIS], it is impossible to ensure either domestic stability or the fight against crime, including drug dealing, weapons contraband and other socially dangerous forms of crimes that are destabilizing to society'. 'Concept of Foreign Policy of the Russian Federation', Russian Federation Ministry of Foreign Affairs Document no. 1615/IS (25 January 1993). Reprinted in FBIS Report FBIS-USR-93-037 (25 March 1993), p. 4.

50 In this case, the high costs of the Russian operation – particularly telling in the general context of economic crisis and underfunding of the defence sector – favoured a Russian shift away from a purely military strategy in Tajikistan and towards political dialogue. See Lena Jonson, *The Tajik War: A Challenge to Russian Policy* Discussion Paper no. 74 (London: The Royal Institute of International Affairs, 1998), pp. 31–32. Jonson rightly situates capability factors within a larger discussion of Russian domestic, regional, and local Tajik developments that together account for the change in Russian policy.

51 See the then Foreign Minister Andrei Kozyrev's advocacy of a leading or 'special' role for Russia in the near abroad, cited in *Segodnya*, 19 January 1994 and February 1 1994.

52 This analogy was specifically drawn by Yevgenii Ambartsumov, then Chairman of the Supreme Soviet's International Affairs Committee, who called in 1992 for a foreign policy doctrine proclaiming 'the entire geopolitical space of the former Union a sphere of vital interests (following the example of the US Monroe Doctrine)'. He stressed further that Russia should obtain international recognition of its role as the guarantor of stability in the former USSR. *Izvestia*, 7 August 1992.

53 Prunier, *The Rwanda Crisis*, pp. 110–111.

54 For a detailed analysis of the role of private military companies, see David Shearer, *Private Armies and Military Intervention*, Adelphi Paper 316 (Oxford: Oxford University Press for the IISS, 1998), pp. 39–55. This discussion draws heavily from Shearer's work.

55 *Ibid.*, p. 48.

56 Jack Straw, 'Foreword', in Foreign and Commonwealth Office, *Private Military Companies: Options for Regulation* (London: The Stationery Office, 2002), p. 4.

Conclusion

1 On the other hand, maintaining strict distinctions between combatants and non-combatants is notoriously difficult in unconventional wars.

2 See John E. Burns, 'US Air Strikes Back Afghan Leader', *International Herald Tribune*, 20 February 2002, p. 3.

3 The UN Charter recognises the

existence of an inherent right of self-defence for member states. Article 51 requires that such acts be reported to the Security Council, but stipulates that 'nothing in the present Charter shall impair the right of individual or collective self-defence'.

4 See Alan Sipress, 'US Still Hasn't Pinned Down the Best Way to Deal with Iraq', *International Herald Tribune*, 20 February 2002, p. 2.